HOW TO CHOOSE A SAILBOAT

How to Choose a Sailboat

by HERVEY GARRETT SMITH

DOUBLEDAY & COMPANY, INC., GARDEN CITY, NEW YORK   1969

By the Same Author

THE RACING SAILOR'S BIBLE
THE SMALL-BOAT SAILOR'S BIBLE
ARTS OF THE SAILOR

Library of Congress Catalog Card Number 78–78694
Copyright © 1969 by Hervey Garrett Smith
Printed in the United States of America
First Edition

Contents

1 Introduction: Different Needs, Different Boats

Choosing and acquiring a new boat is one of the most rewarding experiences a sailor can have. And it is an experience that will probably recur several times in his life.

From the carefree days of adolescence in the first little sailing pram, to the retirement years and the relaxing comfort of a cruising auxiliary, one is always dreaming of "the next boat." Just as a child outgrows his toys, the sailor reaches the point where the boat he loves fulfills his needs no longer, and the time has come to move on to a different type or size.

Choosing a boat is like choosing a wife, with one obvious exception—you can always sell the boat. But it is not a matter to be entered into lightly. It requires careful self-analysis and a step-by-step evaluation of all the factors related to your personal needs and desires.

How many people are involved in your search for a boat? If you are single, with no one to be considered but yourself, your problems are greatly simplified, and your choice of boat is determined by your personal interests and attributes.

The extent of your experience and your sailing ability should be honestly appraised. If you are relatively inexperienced, *don't* consider boats that are designed to be sailed by experts. The high-performance, highly engineered racing craft with their complex rigs are not for you. They are extremely sensitive and hard to handle and will tolerate no mistakes. It takes a skilled crew with extensive experience and training to sail or race them.

You will be happier with a more "whole-some" type, such as the Lightning, Blue Jay, or Celebrity, for example, or any of the numerous day sailer-racers. Competition is just as keen in these classes, and you are more likely to be racing against sailors whose abilities match your own. Get several years' experience before moving up into the "hot" classes and the company of the semipros.

If you have decided to go into cruising, give serious consideration to one of the excellent small, MORC*-type cruising auxiliaries. As a single person you will be dependent upon friends for crew. They may not always be available when you want them, and you will occasionally be sailing singlehanded. The smaller cruising boats with moderate sail area can easily be handled by one man, and with their comparatively simple rigs, sail-handling presents no problems.

For the married couple with children, choosing a boat is more complicated. With a roomy, comfortable day sailer, the whole family can enjoy sailing together. But be forewarned—too much togetherness afloat can often bring complications. To many active youngsters, sailing with Mom and Dad is all right—up to a certain point. But their idea of fun is not quite the same as adults', even their parents'. They can get bored and irritable and would rather look for fun off by themselves or with kids their own age.

Here's where the small, inexpensive fun boats come in. With a little sailing pram or board-boat, the kids can have a barrel

* Midget Ocean Racing Club.

of fun of their own choosing, with their own kind.

For the same reason, the family cruising auxiliary should have a tender with a sailing rig and a small outboard. Cooped up with grown-ups for hours at a time on a cruise, youngsters often have a hard time keeping occupied or amused. But when the hook is down at the end of the day's run, they can rig up the dink, shove off by themselves, and go exploring. With the kids out of the way, the grown-ups can relax over a cocktail, clean up the boat, and prepare a fine dinner without distraction. So give serious thought to becoming a "two-boat family."

Another aspect of choosing a family boat concerns the distaff side. A man can slam into head seas by the hour in a long beat to windward, get soaked to the skin, chilled to the bone, and muscle-weary, and call it fun. But a woman can take this up to a certain point, and then she has *had* it! It's just not her idea of fun. And so, whether it is a day sailer or cruising auxiliary, a fast, wet boat is not prescribed as a steady diet for females.

Women appreciate comfort when sailing, and they're more likely to achieve it in a boat with generous beam, moderate sail area, and enough freeboard and deck space to sail dry. The cockpit should be large enough for several people to relax in without interfering with sail-handling or the operation of the boat. With some of the offshore cruising auxiliaries, there seems to be great emphasis on racing performance and speed. Every man likes a boat that is a smart sailer, but if you're looking for family cruising comfort, speed

is a relative thing, and not an important requisite.

One of the most enjoyable aspects of sailing is gunkholing—exploring out-of-the-way coves and creeks away from traffic and noise, finding a peaceful spot for anchoring off by yourself. Most of these places are accessible only to shoal-draft boats. There are many salt-water bays, estuaries, and inland waterways around our coasts where the water is spread pretty thin, and you'll find that most of the boats draw no more than three or three and a half feet. Boats drawing four or five feet must therefore stick to buoyed channels. Therefore, if you haven't already done so, check the controlling depths of the waters in which you intend to sail.

A good boat trailer can enable you to get the maximum enjoyment out of your boat. It brings distant waters within your reach and widens the horizon. If you have hitherto thought of trailering as confined to small day sailers and racing craft, take note that the size of the boat that can be trailed is limited only to its beam. You can trail your cruising auxiliary anywhere if its beam is no more than eight feet.

One family trailed their 26-footer more than a thousand miles to Florida, and cruised the Florida Keys and returned home, all in a two-week vacation. And they slept in their boat en route. By trailering your boat, you avoid the problem of obtaining a mooring, and you can sail wherever you like. Even if your leisure time is limited, your sailing is not restricted to home waters. And so, if you're looking for a small cruising auxiliary, give thought to a trailer.

2 Construction

The majority of sailboats today are built of molded fiberglass, primarily because the material is so well adapted to mass production. The traditional framed-and-planked wood construction is rapidly being phased out, and its use is confined mainly to large custom-built craft. Some of the high-performance planing boats in the one-design racing classes are built of molded plywood, giving a monocoque-shell of great strength-to-weight ratio. Many of the hard-chine racing craft are still planked with sheet plywood, but these too are gradually switching to fiberglass.

Strip-built hulls, in which narrow wood strips are edge-nailed and glued, are found in a number of small auxiliaries. Like the molded plywood and molded-fiberglass hulls, strip-built construction employs no frames, is very strong and light, and requires a minimum of maintenance.

From the standpoint of engineering and design, the complex systems of compound curves that are peculiar to sailing craft are very easy to develop in fiberglass. The traditional planked wooden boats, on the other hand, require complicated framing and hundreds of fastenings to maintain stiffness of structure and to prevent working and leaking under stress.

The paramount virtue of fiberglass construction is the greatly reduced maintenance—and the bigger the boat the more important this virtue becomes. The owner of a wooden boat generally worries about deterioration and spends many hours in preventive measures. Fiberglass plastic is immune to worms and teredos, dry rot, corrosion, and electrolysis, and there are no calked seams to develop leaks.

One question commonly asked is whether fiberglass boats are susceptible to heat or cold. This question arises from familiarity with thermoplastic products such as garden hose, which gets hard and brittle when cold, and limp or soft in high temperatures.

The polyester resin used in laminating fiberglass boats is not so affected. It actually shows a small increase in strength as the temperature drops far below freezing, and yet, when it is subjected to heat, there is no measurable loss of strength until the temperature rises to about 200° F.

As proof of performance in temperature extremes, the DEW Line radar installations in the far north are housed in fiberglass-reinforced plastic domes. And at the other extreme, the nose cones of missiles employ the same material to withstand the searing heat they are subjected to.

Fiberglass plastic has a high strength-to-weight ratio, and the seamless one-piece hull does not need the heavy framing of wooden boats to maintain stiffness. It also has a low modulus of stiffness, compared to wood and metals, and therefore has high-impact energy-absorbing qualities. In Coast Guard tests, fully loaded lifeboats were dropped from ten feet into the water with little or no damage.

In numerous instances where fiberglass boats have been involved in collisions, the hulls have been deeply dented or deflected under the heavy impact but have popped back to their original shape with no damage other than abrasion of the surface finish. Of course, if there were interior bulkheads at the point of impact, some structural damage could be expected.

MAINTENANCE

While many of the arduous maintenance chores that plague the boat owner have been eliminated, fiberglass boats do require a certain amount of periodic attention to keep them looking their best. Maintenance might be described as a cosmetic problem rather than the repair of structural deterioration.

The outside surface color coat of resin is called the "gel coat" and is only about fifteen mils in thickness. In normal wear and tear the finish can become marred by abrasion or scratched and gouged from a heavy impact. Restoration of the original gloss, as with an automobile finish, involves the use of cleaners and waxes made expressly for fiberglass.

Where color pigments are incorporated in the gel coat, you can expect some fading and chalking. Sunlight is the worst enemy of pigments, and the darker the color the more it will fade. Because it is not truly a color, white gives the longest service. Exposure to sun and weather gradually erodes the surface coat of resin, and a chalky film sloughs off. As far as can be determined, three to five years seems to be the average life expectancy of the gel coat.

At some point in the life of a fiberglass boat the finish becomes so marred or discolored that cleaners and waxes are no longer effective, and it must be painted. Although any regular alkyd marine paint may be used, epoxy enamels or the newer poly-silicones are preferred. The epoxy paints are harder and longer wearing than regular boat paints, and seasonal repainting is unnecessary. Five years seems to be the average life of this coating.

The bottom of a fiberglass boat that is kept in salt water will foul just as readily as a wood boat unless properly protected. While worms or borers will not penetrate fiberglass, algae, grass, and barnacles will attach themselves to the hull. There are antifouling paints especially formulated for fiberglass, and their application requires careful preparation of the surface, otherwise peeling may occur. There is wax on the surface of the fiberglass originating from the molding operation, an invisible film which must be completely removed to get a proper bond. Therefore, before applying antifouling paint, *read the instructions on the can.*

There have been a number of cases where the owners of fiberglass cruising boats have been bothered by condensation on the interior of the hulls. Because of the density of the material, fiberglass hulls are more prone to sweating than wooden ones. This is not a universal problem, however. It occurs from moist, warm air on the inside of the boat coming into contact with the cooler hull surface, which is promoted by low water temperature. Sweating occurs, therefore, only in northern waters in the summer.

Many builders of stock fiberglass auxiliaries have recognized the possibility of sweating and have employed antisweat sheathings. The best, and most commonly used, is a foam-backed vinyl padding or fabric, applied to the interior of the hull with a pressure-sensitive adhesive. Besides serving as an insulating feature, it deadens sound transmission and enhances the appearance of the living area. If the cruising boat of your choice does not have this interior treatment, you can apply it yourself, for this foam fabric can be obtained from many sources.

DURABILITY

Many prospective boat owners are concerned about durability. How long will a fiberglass boat last? Will it maintain its strength after years of hard usage, or does the resin undergo physical changes of a deteriorating nature?

It is a well-known fact that many boats of traditional wooden construction, that have been well built and properly maintained, are still in active service after thirty, forty, or fifty years. There is as yet *no evidence* to support the belief that fiberglass boats cannot equal or better this performance record. Year by year, quality, design, and performance have been improved, through advanced techniques and better materials.

QUALITY

It is very difficult for the average boat buyer to judge accurately the quality of a fiberglass boat. The peculiarities of fiberglass construction almost defy critical examination by the layman.

Bilges are concealed by one-piece, molded-in flooring, and structural reinforcements inside the hull may be hidden by side panels or splatter paint. Your critique therefore is primarily based on appearance.

The interior finish should have comparable quality with the exterior finish. All interior and exterior trim should reveal careful joinery and finish. Deck and cockpit floor should be rigid when stepped on, with no sign of deflection or sponginess. All hardware should be of first quality, and this is of critical importance if the boat is to be used in salt water.

In the final analysis, your best criterion is the experience and reputation of the builder.

3 Fun Boats

The smallest, simplest, and least expensive sailboats are those popularly classed as fun boats. In size they run from seven to about thirteen feet in overall length, with a single sail and unstayed mast. They come in a variety of hull forms, with round, flat, or V-bottoms, from the traditional dinghy or pram to the popular board-boat, which doesn't even look like a boat. Practically all of them have built-in flotation and will remain afloat when capsized or full of water.

Safe and easy to handle, these are the types to consider when choosing a youngster's first boat. Being light in weight and simply rigged, they are easily transported by cartop or trailer, and a boy can launch and rig one in minutes.

A boat of this type is very sensitive and responsive to the helm, and with a single sheet to handle, a youngster soon learns how to make the boat go where he wants it to. With the aptitude and inquisitiveness of the very young, in a short time he will acquire an understanding of the basic elements of sailing and seamanship, and above all, he will develop self-reliance.

Inevitably there comes the first informal brush with another boat, and he becomes aware that racing is another aspect of sailing fun. Many fun boats have active class organizations for local, area, and national competition. Here he can compete against youngsters of his own age and experience, most of them beginners like himself.

While racing is fun, the rewards are even greater. A beginner will learn more in one race about handling a sailboat than he would in a week of aimlessly sailing around by himself. A competitor starts to pass him and he wonders why. He experiments by shifting his weight, and notices the effect of slacking off or trimming in the sail. He has a compelling urge to make the boat go faster, and he learns how by watching the other fellow. Soon he is absorbed in racing rules and tactics, and all the while he's getting training in seamanship and becoming imbued in sportsmanship of the highest order. A couple of seasons and he has outgrown the little fun boat and is ready for something more challenging—a boat of higher performance, whose handling demands greater proficiency in those skills he has recently acquired.

BUCKEYE

Length overall 12'8"
Length at waterline 12'1"
Beam 4'11"
Draft 3'3", centerboard down
Sail area 101 square feet
Weight 190 pounds

The Buckeye is a sturdy little fiberglass sloop for family fun at the beach or camp. She is a comfortable day sailer for two adults or three youngsters, and is sporty enough for informal racing. Fast and responsive, with boom vang and track-mounted jib sheet leads, she is an excellent boat for junior training, or as a youngster's first boat. Light enough to be cartopped.

Royal Sailboats Company
4983 Reed Road
Columbus, Ohio 43221

19

D

CLASS D DYER DINK

Length overall 10'
Beam 4'3"
Sail area 66 square feet
Weight 135 pounds

The Class D Dyer Dink has for years been used in intercollegiate, yacht club junior and senior programs, and in Frostbite championships. Very popular as a tender for ocean racing yachts. Fiberglass hull has built-in flotation, and is fitted with rowlocks for rowing. The spruce spars fit within the boat for easy transporting by cartop or trailer.

The Anchorage, Inc.
57 Miller Street
Warren, Rhode Island 02885

9' DYER DHOW

Length overall 9'
Beam 4'5"
Sail area 45 square feet
Weight 104 pounds

The fiberglass Dyer Dhows with their patented hull form are known the world over. Thousands of youngsters have learned to sail in them, and Frostbiting owes its popularity to them. The loose-footed cat rig is easy to handle, and the spars stow within the boat. She can be powered with an outboard or rowed, has flotation blocks under the seats, and is an ideal yacht tender. Camps and yacht clubs use Dyer Dhows for junior training and racing.

The Anchorage, Inc.
57 Miller Street
Warren, Rhode Island 02885

D
D

12½' DYER DHOW

Length overall 12'6"
Beam 60"
Sail area 91 square feet

Originally designed for use at the West Point Military Academy, this boat is excellent for class racing at yacht clubs, schools, or camps. With two maststeps, she can be rigged as a cat or sloop. Roomy and very able, you can race her alone or take the whole family day sailing. The fiberglass hull has flotation blocks under the seats, and is light enough to cartop. With an outboard and oars, she is a versatile yacht tender.

The Anchorage, Inc.
57 Miller Street
Warren, Rhode Island 02885

EL TORO

Length overall 7'10½"
Beam 46"
Sail area 37.5 square feet
Weight 85 pounds

El Toro has been steadily gaining in popularity as a one-man racing class and day sailer, and now numbers over six thousand boats, mainly on the Pacific Coast. She is a hard-chine pram available in either mahogany plywood or fiberglass. With built-in flotation, she is a fine boat for children, and without the sailing rig, can be rowed or powered by a small outboard. Has grooved spruce spars, and is rigged with a boom vang. Light enough to be loaded on cartop by one man.

W. D. Schock Company
3502 South Greenville Street
Santa Ana, California 92704

NAPLES SABOT

Length overall 7′10″
Beam 48″
Sail area 36 square feet
Weight 85 pounds

The Naples Sabot is a sailing/rowing pram with leeboards, a fun boat for children or adults. The fiberglass hull has integrally molded flotation tanks. Spars are spruce or aluminum, and the sail is loosefooted. Transom can take a small outboard up to 3 hp. This inexpensive little boat can be car-topped or carried in a station wagon.

W. D. Schock Company
3502 South Greenville Street
Santa Ana, California 92704

ROOTERS

Length overall 9'7"
Beam 46"
Sail area 37 square feet
Weight 65 pounds

This little hard-chine plywood sailboat with a lateen sail offers one-design class racing for youngsters at a minimum cost. The hull is that of a typical flat-bottom sharpie with a daggerboard. The mast is unstayed, so the sail can be let run all the way forward to prevent capsizing in a heavy puff. This is an excellent first boat for one or two kids. She can be carried in a station wagon or cartopped. Plans are available for home builders, and construction is very simple.

Rooster Boat Company
Hawthorne Road
Jamestown, Rhode Island 02835

S-12

Length overall 12'
Beam 48"
Sail area 75 square feet
Weight 178 pounds

The S-12 is a cat-rigged sailboat with a fiberglass scow-type hull, popular on the Inland Lakes. She can be used for racing or as a fun boat. She has a shallow well-type cockpit, a pivoting aluminum center-board, and is easily righted if capsized. Spars are aluminum and sail is nylon. A jib kit is available if a sloop rig is desired. The boat can be cartopped or trailered.

Aluma Craft Boat Division
Alpex Corporation
1515 Central Avenue N.E.
Minneapolis, Minnesota 55413

SAILFISH

Length overall 11′7½″
Beam 31½″
Weight 82 pounds
Sail area 65 square feet
Crew capacity 300 pounds

SUPER SAILFISH

Length overall 13′7″
Beam 35½″
Weight 102 pounds
Sail area 75 square feet
Crew capacity 400 pounds

The Sailfish is a board-boat of molded fiberglass or plywood. She is strictly a fun boat for the young-at-heart, the bathing suit set, and the beaches. Since the boat is unsinkable, capsizing is commonplace and part of the fun. She can be righted and under way again in a matter of seconds. Racing a Sailfish is exciting, for she planes easily in moderate breezes. With a spring-loaded daggerboard and a flip-up rudder, she can be sailed right into the beach. Rigging and unrigging takes but a minute, and the boat can easily be cartopped.

AMF Alcort
P.O. Box 1345
Waterbury, Connecticut 06720

SUNFISH

Length overall 13'10"
Beam 48½"
Weight 139 pounds
Sail area 75 square feet
Crew capacity 500 pounds

The Sunfish is much like the Sailfish, but with a foot more beam and two feet more length, and the addition of a foot-well or cockpit, she is more of a family boat. Also unsinkable, she is a smart sailer and very fast. As a racing class she offers keen competition all over the world, and over fifty thousand are registered. While she can be cartopped, a specially designed trailer is available. Factory-finished boats are fiberglass, but plywood kits can be furnished.

AMF Alcort
P.O. Box 1345
Waterbury, Connecticut 06720

SCORPION

Length overall 13'9"
Beam 3'11½"
Sail area 75 square feet

The Scorpion is a fiberglass board-boat used as a fun boat for day sailing and for racing. She is unsinkable, and is easily righted when capsized. The skipper sits in a shallow well or cockpit, which keeps his weight low and adds stability. The lateen sail has aluminum spars. Light in weight, she can be carried in a station wagon or on top of the car.

Columbia Car Corporation
4300 Raleigh Street
Charlotte, North Carolina 28205

S

SNOWBIRD

Length overall 12'
Beam 5'
Sail area 102 square feet
Weight 275 pounds

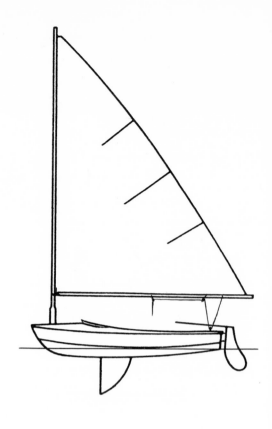

One of the largest and best-known racing classes in the Pacific Southwest, the Snowbird is a monotype centerboard day sailer and racer for kids or adults. Spars are spruce, and the fiberglass hull has built-in flotation. She has bow and side decks, which keep out spray. A good single-hander, or can take four in comfort. She is easily trailered.

W. D. Schock Company
3502 South Greenville Street
Santa Ana, California 92704

SWIFT

Length overall 10'4"
Beam 3'2"
Weight 80 pounds
Sail area 44 square feet
Crew capacity 300 pounds

SUPER SWIFT

Length overall 12'8"
Beam 3'8"
Weight 120 pounds
Sail area 80 square feet
Crew capacity 500 pounds

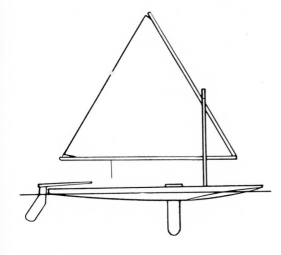

The Swift and Super Swift are sailboards, identical except in size. They have positive flotation, a self-bailing recessed cockpit, and kick-up rudder. They can be car-topped, and require but little space for storage. The Super Swift is very popular for racing, and can provide plenty of thrills.

The O'Day Corporation
168 Stevens Street
Fall River, Massachusetts 02722

OTHER FUN BOATS

CAPE DORY 10
10'6"×4'1"×2'5". Sail area 68 square feet. Cat rig. Hull weight 145 pounds. Fiberglass hull, aluminum spars. Accommodates three. Positive flotation.

Cape Dory Company
373 Crescent Street
West Bridgewater, Massachusetts 02379

INTERCLUB
11'6"×4'7"×3'. Sail area 72 square feet. Cat rig. Hull weight 195 pounds. Fiberglass hull, aluminum spars. Positive flotation. Accommodates two or three.

The O'Day Corporation
168 Stevens Street
Fall River, Massachusetts 02722

JOLLY BOAT DINGHY
8'4"×4'2"×1'9". Sail area 56 square feet. Cat rig. Hull weight 80 pounds. Fiberglass hull, aluminum spars. Positive flotation.

S. S. Brandon Manufacturing and
England Company
2905B SW Second Avenue
Ft. Lauderdale, Florida 33315

KINGFISHER
11'6"×4'8"×2'2". Sail area 75 square feet. Lateen rig. Fiberglass hull, aluminum spars. Positive flotation, self-righting. Accommodates two or three.

Atlantic Laminates, Inc.
2506 Merrick Road
Bellmore, New York 11710

SCAMPER 11
11'×3'. Sail area 48 square feet. Lateen rig. Hull weight 40 pounds. Expanded Polystyrene hull, aluminum spars. Unsinkable. Crew capacity, 400 pounds.

Formex Corporation
505 Belvedere Road
Elkhart, Indiana 46514

SEA SCOUTER
10'×4'4"×22". Sail area 60 square feet. Cat rig. Fiberglass hull, aluminum spars. Hull weight 112 pounds. Accommodates three people. Nonsinkable.

Youth Adventure, Inc.
238 Central Building
Seattle, Washington

SEA SNARK
11'×3'2". Sail area 45 square feet. Lateen rig. Hull weight 30 pounds. Expanded Polystyrene hull, aluminum spars. Unsinkable.

Snark Products, Inc.
1580 Lemoine Avenue
Fort Lee, New Jersey 07024

4 Day Sailers

In its ideal concept, the day sailer is a small sailboat under twenty feet, safe and easy to handle, in which a family can while away the daylight hours in relaxed, comfortable sailing. In choosing such a boat for family fun, you should be on the lookout for a number of important characteristics, all having a direct bearing on your enjoyment.

First, the boat should have good initial stability, ample beam, and a moderate sail area. This insures ease of handling, peace of mind, and comfort. A boat that is tender and requires constant shifting of live weight to maintain balance is not a comfortable sailer. If the whole crew has to hike out on the weather rail to keep the boat upright in the puffs, you will not have relaxed sailing. And don't be influenced by a boat's reputed speed—as far as sailboats are concerned, speed is relative. The very fast, high-performance boats demand constant, precise handling and instant reflexes. You sail under tension and cannot relax for a moment.

A good day sailer should have a large cockpit, preferably with seats, so that you sit *in* rather than *on* the boat. A forward deck is desirable because it keeps out the spray and provides a dry place to stow your belongings. Practically all small sailboats have (or *should* have) built-in flotation, so that they will float when filled with water. Some are designed to be self-righting in the event of a capsizal.

In recent years the day sailer has been developed far beyond the original concept, and it has greater utility. Many day sailers are used for racing and have well-organized class associations, local and national. There are also a number of day sailer-cruisers, with limited accommodations for weekend cruising or overnight trips. They'll have a couple of berths, a head, and space for a galley. With a small outboard clamped on the stern, you have a midget cruising auxiliary. Many youngsters have had glorious adventures "cruising" in a twelve-footer, with sleeping bags and a cockpit awning over the boom.

Some boats that were designed primarily for racing are also excellent day sailers. One example is the Lightning. It has a large cockpit, ample decks, and good initial stability. For two adults and one or too small fry, it is a good family boat as well as a smart racing boat.

Nothing has done more to increase the popularity of the day sailer than the trailer. It has brought sailing within reach of people who live hundreds of miles from navigable water. It widens the scope of your activity, and you can trail your boat to different waters every weekend. When you leave for a vacation, your boat goes with you, be it a hundred or a thousand miles away.

A trailer pays off in dollars and cents as well as in greater utility. You avoid expensive mooring or docking fees and you eliminate boatyard bills. Your boat can be stored in your own backyard, and since it is out of water a good part of the time, antifouling bottom paint is unnecessary and maintenance is reduced to a minimum.

With such a wide variety of boats available, choosing a day sailer intelligently requires a careful analysis of your personal requirements and the factors involved— age, amount of experience, scope of recreational interests, size of family or number of participants, and your budget.

BUTTERFLY

Length overall 12'
Beam 54"
Sail area 75 square feet
Weight 150 pounds
Crew capacity 600 pounds

The cat-rigged Butterfly scow is patterned after the popular Class C inland lake scow, with a daggerboard instead of twin bilge boards. The fiberglass hull is unsinkable. The aluminum mast pivots on deck, and the rudder is the kick-up type. Butterfly is a fine family fun boat, light enough to be cartopped, launched, and rigged by one person. She has a 24×45-inch foot-well, and can carry four adults. She planes easily, and is very fast in a strong breeze. A very popular one-design racing class in the Midwest.

Barnett Boat Co.
Route 3, Box 500A
Kenosha, Wisconsin 53140

CELEBRITY

Length overall 19'9"
Length at waterline 15'9"
Beam 6'4"
Draft 3'3"
Sail area 172 square feet

Built of molded mahogany, the Celebrity is a handsome day sailer-racer with the "feel" of a much larger boat. Available in both centerboard and fin-keel models, she is fast, weatherly in a stiff breeze, and has good stability. With an inboard rudder and large afterdeck, the boat has the crew weight amidships for better balance. Six to eight can be carried for day sailing without overcrowding. Mast is hollow spruce, and boom has roller reefing. A portable canvas spray-shield is available, which can be rigged as a shelter cabin for sleeping. The Celebrity is very well built and beautifully finished.

P. Evanson Boat Company
Reserve Avenue
Riverside, New Jersey 08075

DS

DAY SAILER

Length overall 16'9"
Length at waterline 16'
Beam 6'3"
Draft 3'9" centerboard down
Sail area 145 square feet
Weight 600 pounds

This is one of the most popular family sail-boats for its size. The fiberglass hull has positive foam flotation built in. Room in the cockpit for six. The cuddy cabin makes for a dry boat, and provides ample stowage space. Ideal for youngsters, she is easily trailered, and many are raced. Has an outboard well; with a tent over the boom, she can be used by kids for overnight cruising. More than thirty-eight hundred of these boats are in use.

The O'Day Corporation
168 Stevens Street
Fall River, Massachusetts 02722

GEMINI

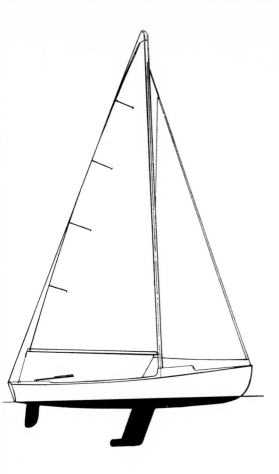

Length overall 16'1"
Length at waterline 14'9"
Beam 5'7"
Draft 40" centerboard down
Sail area 140 square feet
Weight 440 pounds

The fiberglass Gemini has a planing hull with twin centerboards, designed and built for fleet racing. The twin boards are installed at the angle of average heel, resulting in less wetted surface and faster sailing. With ample decks and small cuddy cabin, she sails dry. Cockpit is comfortable, there is ample flotation, and spars are aluminum with roller reefing. This is a good training boat for youngsters, and a good family day sailer. She is easily trailered, and can be fitted for an outboard.

Cape Cod Shipbuilding Company
Narrows Road
Wareham, Massachusetts 02571

GOLDENEYE

Length overall 18'3"
Length at waterline 15'10"
Beam 6'4"
Draft 3'
Sail area 193 square feet
Displacement 2500 pounds
Ballast keel 1320 pounds

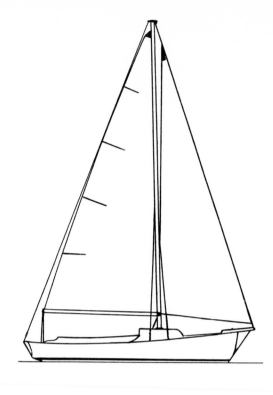

While this little keel sloop is primarily a family day sailer, she can also be used for overnight or weekend cruising. Under the cuddy cabin and forward deck are two berths molded in, and a toilet may be installed. The cockpit is self-bailing, and large enough for relaxing with comfort. The masthead rig and short bowsprit permit a good-sized genoa. Spars are aluminum with roller reefing.

Cape Cod Shipbuilding Company
Narrows Road
Wareham, Massachusetts 02571

JAVELIN

Length overall 14'
Beam 5'8"
Draft 3'10"
Centerboard model 2'
Sail area 125 square feet, keel model

Javelin is a versatile day sailer or racer with good stability, ample beam, and a very roomy cockpit. She has built-in flotation, and is available in either keel or centerboard model. Besides the working sails, she carries a spinnaker, and will plane in a stiff breeze. Ideal beginner's boat for youngsters. Outboard up to 5 hp can be carried on the transom.

The O'Day Corporation
168 Stevens Street
Fall River, Massachusetts 02722

MOUETTE

Length overall 19'6"
Length at waterline 18'
Beam 6'11"
Maximum draft 4'
Sail area 165 square feet
Weight 640 pounds

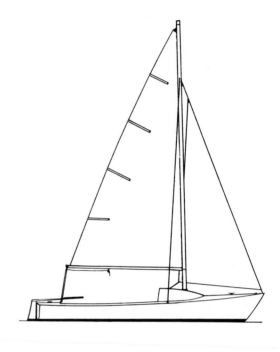

This is an excellent family day sailer for adults or juniors, with a fiberglass planing hull and positive foam flotation. The large self-bailing cockpit seats four or five comfortably, and the cuddy cabin gives shelter from flying spray. A spinnaker and genoa jib are optional extras. She has an outboard motor well, is fitted with hiking straps, and has a kick-up rudder. With a moderate sail area, she is a very able performer, easy to handle and safe for kids.

Paceship, division of
Industrial Shipping Company, Ltd.
Mahone Bay, Nova Scotia, Canada

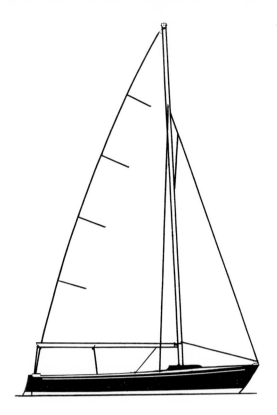

MUSTANG 17

Length overall 17′
Length at waterline 15′5″
Beam 6′6″
Draft 47″
Sail area 170 square feet
Weight 700 pounds

The Mustang fiberglass sloop was designed for family day sailing, one-design racing, or junior training. A heavily ballasted centerboard, self-bailing cockpit, and foam flotation make the boat self-righting in the event of a capsizal. In racing she carries a genoa jib and spinnaker, and will plane off the wind. With a large, wide cockpit, up to six people can be accommodated for day sailing. Cockpit seats are optional.

Annapolis Boat Rentals, Inc.
P.O. Box 1669
Annapolis, Maryland 21404

OSPRAY

Length overall 15′8″
Beam 5′11″
Draft 3′8″
Sail area 125 square feet
Weight 480 pounds

Ospray is a comfortable day sailer with a long cockpit that can seat six. Small shelter cabin and long forward deck keeps out spray and provides stowage space for lunches and spare gear. She is light enough to trail and launch easily, has a well for mounting an outboard. Rigged to sail with a spinnaker. The Ospray is no longer made.

The O'Day Corporation
168 Stevens Street
Fall River, Massachusetts 02722

42

PEREGRINE 16

Length overall 15′7″
Beam 6′
Maximum draft 42″
Sail area 128 square feet
Weight 425 pounds

The Peregrine 16 was designed primarily for youngsters, and for club sailing and racing programs. The one-piece fiberglass hull has positive foam flotation, and the cockpit is self-bailing. The enclosed cuddy provides stowage space for gear and keeps the boat dry in heavy weather. This is a sporty boat—lively, fast, and sensitive, and an excellent trainer. For racing, a spinnaker and genoa jib can be had as an extra. There is a motor well aft to take a light outboard and the boat is easily trailered.

Paceship, division of
Industrial Shipping Company, Ltd.
Mahone Bay, Nova Scotia, Canada

PINTAIL

Length overall 14'
Beam 6'
Draft 6" to 48"
Sail area 122 square feet
Weight 400 pounds

The Pintail is a versatile, smart-sailing fiberglass sloop, equally suitable for family day sailing, junior training programs, and racing. As a one-design racing boat, she has a planing hull, and flies a spinnaker. The cockpit is roomy and the ample deck keeps her dry. With good initial stability and a well-balanced rig, she is easy to handle and a pleasure to sail.

MFG Boat
P.O. Box 312
Union City, Pennsylvania 16438

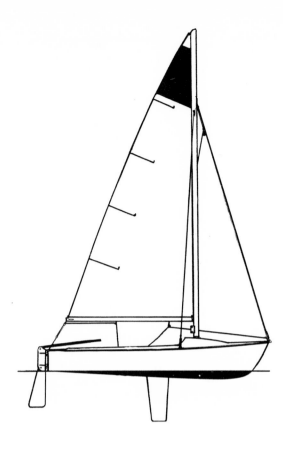

REDHEAD

Length overall 17′3″
Beam 6′1″
Sail area 178 square feet
Weight 600 pounds

This all-fiberglass centerboarder is a stiff and able family day sailer. The roomy cockpit has full-length seats, and is self-bailing and self-rescuing, with built-in flotation. The raised deck provides weather protection for gear and passengers. The boat has a rotating gold-anodized aluminum mast stepped on deck, roller reefing, and kick-up rudder. Outboard motor well is molded in. An ideal boat for two adults and a couple of youngsters, safe and easy to handle.

MFG Boat
P.O. Box 312
Union City, Pennsylvania 16438

45

RELIANCE

Length overall 21'4"
Length at waterline 17'8"
Beam 6'9"
Draft: centerboard up, 1'9";
    centerboard down, 3'6"
Sail area 182 square feet

The Reliance is a fiberglass keel-centerboard day sailer, with a cast-iron ballast keel housing a centerboard. With wide decks, a 9-foot-long cockpit, and plenty of stowage space, she is an excellent family boat for open waters. The aluminum mast is hinged on deck for lowering to go under bridges and for trailering.

Annapolis Boat Rentals, Inc.
P.O. Box 1669
Annapolis, Maryland 21404

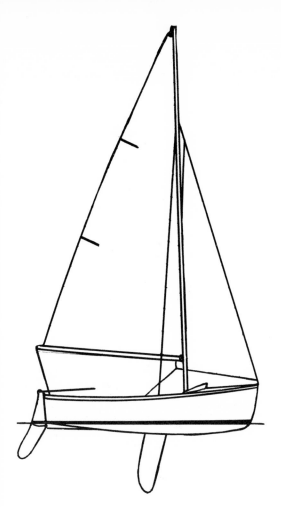

ROBIN

Length overall 10'10"
Length at waterline 10'3½"
Beam 4'8"
Sail area 80 square feet

This little sailboat is versatile—she can be sailed as a sloop or catboat, powered with an outboard, or rowed. As a sloop she is fast enough for the experienced sailor to race. As a catboat she is ideal for the beginner or for training youngsters. Now available in either fiberglass or molded plywood, she has built-in flotation and is unsinkable. She is light enough to be carried on the top of your car—even a Volkswagen.

P. Evanson Boat Company, Inc.
Reserve Avenue
Riverside, New Jersey 08075

7/11

SEVEN-ELEVEN

Length overall 7′11″
Beam 4′2″
Sail area 34 square feet
Draft 2′4″ centerboard down

Seven-Eleven is an ideal yacht tender and family fun boat. Fiberglass with positive foam flotation, and vinyl gunwhale guard. She can be rowed or powered with up to 3-hp outboard. Aluminum spars can be stowed inside the hull for traveling. Light enough to be hoisted aboard a larger boat.

The O'Day Corporation
168 Stevens Street
Fall River, Massachusetts 02722

48

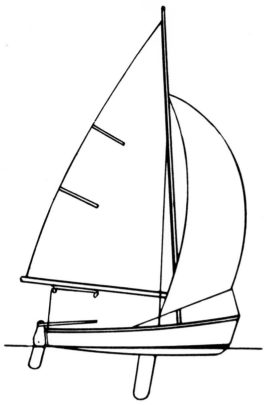

SPRITE

Length overall 10'2"
Beam 4'9"
Draft 3'5" centerboard down
Sail area 63 square feet
Weight 150 pounds

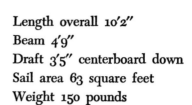

Sprite is a fast-moving, lively little sailboat for three or four youngsters or one or two adults. She can be sailed cat-rigged, or changed to a sloop by moving the mast aft and hoisting the jib. You can even carry a spinnaker. Has kick-up rudder and a pivoted centerboard. This is a good boat for frostbiting, or for training small fry.

The O'Day Corporation
168 Stevens Street
Fall River, Massachusetts 02722

49

T

TEMPEST
(INTERNATIONAL)

Length overall 21'11¾"
Length at waterline 19'3"
Beam 6'5½"
Draft 3'7"
Sail area 247 square feet
Weight 1035 pounds

One of the most advanced designs in recent years, this two-man keel boat is a highly engineered racing machine. She is extremely close-winded, and proper utilization of the trapeze and bending mast allow the boat to be raced in almost any weather. She is a boat for experienced sailors only, and they must have physical agility and quick reflexes to compete successfully. The hull has three separate air compartments, and the cockpit is self-bailing, even when heeled. The 505-pound keel may be retracted for trailering.

The O'Day Corporation
168 Stevens Street
Fall River, Massachusetts 02722

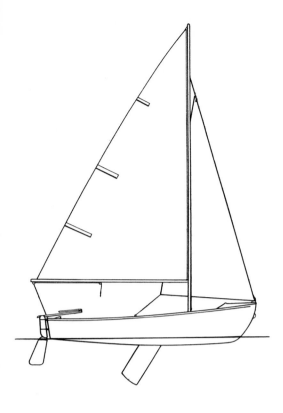

WHISTLER

Length overall 11'
Beam 5'
Sail area 74 square feet
Weight 200 pounds

This little fiberglass sloop with a loose-footed mainsail has two mast steps, so that she can be sailed as a catboat if it is desired, which is heartily recommended for beginners. She is an exceptionally fine boat for junior training, family use, or racing. She has the smart sailing performance of a much larger boat, and can provide thrilling fun with safety for youngsters and adults alike. The cockpit is roomy for a boat this size, and has built-in flotation.

MFG Boat
P.O. Box 312
Union City, Pennsylvania 16438

WIDGEON

Length overall 12′4″
Beam 5′
Draft 3′6″ centerboard down
Sail area 90 square feet
Weight 250 pounds

Widgeon is an ideal boat for camps, for junior training, or for parents to sail with their children. She can be sailed with the mainsail only, since she has an adjustable centerboard. She has built-in flotation, and is easily cartopped or trailered. Spars are foam-filled aluminum.

The O'Day Corporation
168 Stevens Street
Fall River, Massachusetts 02722

PUFFIN
14′×6′×2′6″. Sail area 102 square feet.
Spinnaker optional. Fiberglass hull,
aluminum spars. Positive flotation.
Races with crew of two. The Puffin is no
longer made.

The O'Day Corporation
168 Stevens Street
Fall River, Massachusetts 02722

5   Racing Boats, Including Multihulls

Since man first sailed the seven seas, he has had the competitive urge to pit his skill against his fellow seamen, to sail his ship faster and beat the others into port. To be sure, he was motivated by the possibility of profit rather than fun, but the sporting aspect was there, nonetheless. Today, organized yacht racing offers competitive fun to all sailors, be they eight years old or eighty, from the tyro to the international expert.

Choosing a racing boat is therefore a matter of deciding which class offers the type of competition you desire. The dominant factors are age and experience. A ten-year-old wants to race against kids his age, and a fifty-year-old would feel embarrassed in a class predominantly raced by teenagers.

As an example of how this is taken care of in one class, the Blue Jays are raced in three divisions. Sailors under fifteen race in the Midgets, over fifteen but under eighteen are in the Junior division, and the Open division takes care of the old fogies.

A beginner in racing, be he young or old, should start in a small one-design-class boat that is simply rigged, stable, and easy to handle. After a couple of seasons' experience, he'll have gotten all he can out of the boat and will be ready to move up to a boat with higher performance, where the competition is of higher caliber.

The reason for beginning with a boat suited to your abilities should be obvious. The object in all racing is to win. But if you start racing in a class where the skippers are all experienced experts, it can be mighty discouraging to finish last in every race. Furthermore, you'll learn more and progress more rapidly if you race with those whose experience and abilities match your own.

For the athletically inclined, the high-performance, lightweight, planing-type boats are popular, such as the Jet 14, O.K. Dinghy, or Flying Dutchman. Some planing boats, notably the International Tempest, employ a trapeze. Very fast and exciting to race, they require expert handling, and the crew must be agile and mentally alert and have instant reflexes.

The most spectacular racing boats are the catamarans, which are unlike anything else that sails. In a strong breeze they take off at fantastic speeds, and the harder it blows the faster they go. They have inherent characteristics unlike those of any other boat, and an experienced sailor needs a little practice to handle them properly.

One of the requirements for active participation in one-design-class racing is yacht-club affiliation. The recognized yacht clubs provide the facilities and conduct the races. Aside from the social aspects, and meeting with people who have a common interest, your membership provides activities for you and your family's enjoyment, and insures their continuance for youngsters of the next generation.

In the final analysis, if you are choosing your first racing boat, you would be wise to consider only those that have a strong, active class organization in the area in which you'll be sailing. If a class is consistently gaining popularity in your area, under enthusiastic, aggressive leadership, you can be assured of satisfying competition and maximum fun.

At the other extreme, if you were to buy into a class that is dwindling in numbers locally, you might end up owning an "orphan" that would have a very low resale value.

ALBACORE

Length overall 15'
Beam 5'4"
Draft 4'9" centerboard down
Sail area 125 square feet
Weight 300 pounds

The Albacore is a fast, high-performance planing dinghy, of fiberglass or molded plywood construction, depending on the builder, and has built-in flotation. Having a forward deck, she is a dry boat, and can be used as a family day sailer for up to four adults. She is easily trailered and launched. A good boat for training, and carries a spinnaker.

Grampian Marine, Ltd.
451 Woody Road
Oakville, Ontario, Canada

AQUA-CAT

Length overall 12'2"
Beam 6'
Maximum draft 2'
Sail area 90 square feet
Weight 160 pounds

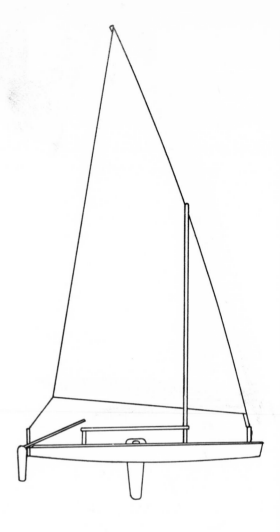

Designed for family fun or exciting competition, this catamaran is easy to sail and safe for youngsters. Her fiberglass hulls are foam-filled, and she's light enough to be cartopped. In racing she has been clocked at over eighteen knots. With sail removed she can be converted to an outboard. Class organization numbers over three thousand in the United States.

American Fiberglass Corporation
Rockland Road
Norwalk, Connecticut 06856

BARNEGAT 17

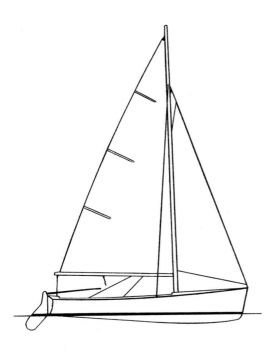

Length overall 16'7"
Length at waterline 16'2"
Beam 6'
Sail area 145 square feet

This fiberglass sloop was designed for family day sailing and racing. Easy to handle, with a roomy cockpit, she can be day sailed by four or five in comfort. With racing sails, including spinnaker, the experienced racing skipper will appreciate her high performance. She is lively, moves easily in light airs, and planes in a breeze. She has a metal centerboard for stability, aluminum spars and kick-up rudder. Easy to trail and launch.

Siddons and Sindle, Inc.
17 Central Avenue
Island Heights, New Jersey 08732

B LION

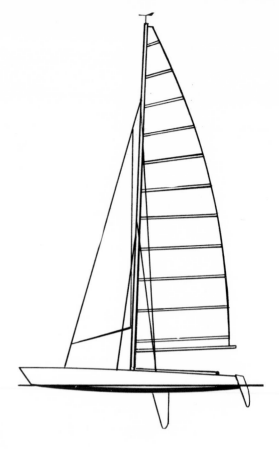

Length overall 20′
Length at waterline 19′
Beam 10′
Maximum draft 2′6″
Sail area 235 square feet
Weight 420 pounds

The B Lion is a sloop-rigged racing catamaran with a full-battened, high-aspect-
ratio mainsail and pivoting aluminum mast.
The fiberglass hulls have kick-up centerboards and rudders. The connecting cross-
beams are hinged in the middle so that the
craft can be folded for trailering. Designed
to International Class B specifications, the
B Lion has won several championships. A
custom trailer is available.

American Fiberglass Corporation
Rockland Road
Norwalk, Connecticut 06856

J

BLUE JAY

Length overall 13'6"
Beam 5'2"
Draft 3'6" centerboard down
Sail area 90 square feet
Weight 275 pounds

With the Class Association now numbering over fifty-one hundred boats, the Blue Jay has achieved national recognition as a racing junior training sloop. Racing with full spinnaker gear, the young sailor gets the sail-handling experience that all modern racing yachts require. Originally built of plywood, the sloop now has fiberglass construction approved by the Class Association. Raced with a crew of two, she is a comfortable day sailer for three.

McNair Marine, Inc.
Killingsworth Road
Route 81
Higganum, Connecticut 06441

CATFISH

Length overall 13'2"
Beam 6'
Weight 190 pounds
Sail area 105 square feet
Crew capacity 300 pounds

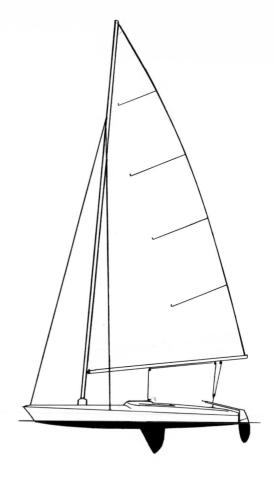

The Catfish is an all-fiberglass catamaran. While she may be used for family fun, she was primarily designed for one-man racing. Heeling and hiking at eighteen or twenty knots provide plenty of thrills. She has built-in flotation, free-feathering aluminum mast, and flip-up rudders. She can be cartopped or trailered, and can be launched, rigged, and ready to sail in under five minutes.

AMF Alcort
P.O. Box 1345
Waterbury, Connecticut 06720

DC-14 P

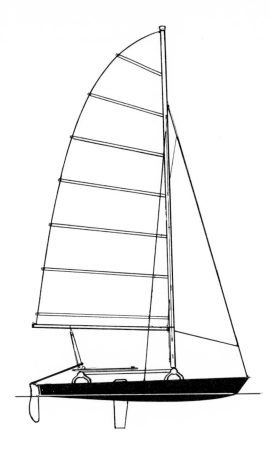

DC-14 PHANTOM

Length overall 14'2"
Beam 7'
Sail area 140 square feet
Weight 350 pounds

The DC-14 is a high-performance sloop-rigged catamaran for fun sailing or racing. The fiberglass hulls and aluminum spars have foam flotation. The mainsail has full-length battens, and the mast is rotating. Has trampoline lounge deck of Dacron, with raised seats each side. Rudders are raised or lowered by pushing or pulling the tiller. The hulls are detachable for car-topping. She has excellent stability, great speed, and is very easy to sail.

Duncan Sutphen, Inc.
342 Madison Avenue
New York, New York 10017

ENSIGN

Length overall 22′6″
Length at waterline 16′9″
Beam 7′
Draft 3′
Sail area 290 square feet
Weight 3000 pounds

With forty-two fleets and fifteen hundred boats in the national class association, the Ensign has proved to be an outstanding racing day sailer. Strictly one-design, this all-fiberglass keel sloop is fast, able, and easy to handle. With a large cockpit and a moderate sail area, she is a very comfortable family day sailer. Under the cuddy cabin and foredeck are two berths and a toilet for overnight or weekend cruising, and foam flotation is provided throughout. An outboard motor can be carried on a transom bracket, and the boat is trailable. As a family boat of maximum utility, the Ensign is one of the best.

Pearson Yachts
West Shore Road
Portsmouth, Rhode Island 02871

ENTERPRISE
(NATIONAL)

Length overall 13'3"
Beam 5'3"
Draft 3'7"
Sail area 113 square feet
Weight 230 pounds

The Enterprise is a high-performance racing dinghy, with a double-chine hull built of wood or fiberglass. Hers is the largest one-design dinghy class in Great Britain, with over two thousand registered. She is very fast, gets on a plane very easily, and is unsinkable. She is raced with a crew of two and can be day sailed with four. Has three cubic feet of stowage space under the foredeck. Kits are available in various stages of completion.

National Enterprise Company
507 Fifth Avenue
New York, New York 10036

FD

FLYING DUTCHMAN

Length overall 19'10"
Beam 5'7"
Draft 3'8"
Sail area 200 square feet
Weight 375 pounds

An Olympic Class two-man centerboarder, the Flying Dutchman is a high-performance racing boat with a planing hull. She employs a trapeze, carries a spinnaker, and attains very high speeds. She is available in either fiberglass or molded plywood construction, and has built-in flotation. The International Class was organized in 1955, and has over four thousand registered owners.

Siddons and Sindle, Inc.
17 Central Avenue
Island Heights, New Jersey 08732

FJ

FLYING JUNIOR

Length overall 13'2"
Length at waterline 12'3"
Beam 5'3"
Maximum draft 34"
Sail area 100 square feet
Weight 259 pounds

The Flying Junior is one of the fastest growing one-design junior racing classes, with twenty-one hundred registered in the United States and seven thousand worldwide. With a simple main and jib rig, this is a very popular club boat for junior training and racing, and is easily trailered. She is fast, lively, and fun to sail. Of one-piece fiberglass construction, she has a self-bailing cockpit, positive foam flotation, and is unsinkable. Spars and centerboard are aluminum, and she has roller reefing.

Paceship, division of
Industrial Shipping Company, Ltd.
Mahone Bay, Nova Scotia, Canada

FLYING SCOT

Length overall 19'
Length at waterline 18'4"
Beam 6'9"
Maximum draft 4'
Sail area 190 square feet

The Flying Scot is one of the finest family day sailer-racers for her size. Her fiberglass hull has positive flotation, and with her very wide decks can be capsized and righted, often without the crew getting their feet wet. She has hard bilges and sufficient beam so that she can be planed without resorting to acrobatics or a trapeze. A 200-square-foot spinnaker is carried, and class rules permit a crew of two, three, or four. There is ample room for six when day sailing. She is very stable, easy to handle, and very fast. Among the accessories listed as available is a genuine "Glengarrie" Scottish bonnet.

Gordon Douglass Boat Company, Inc.
P.O. Box 28
Oakland, Maryland 21550

FLYING TERN

Length overall 14'
Beam 5'3"
Draft 3' centerboard down
Sail area 120 square feet
Weight 286 pounds

The Flying Tern is a fiberglass two-man planing centerboarder for racing, and can carry up to four adults for day sailing. The hull has built-in flotation tanks. With an extra mast step, the boat can be sailed as a cat by moving the mast forward, and eliminating the jib. The racing rig carries a genoa and spinnaker.

Annapolis Boat Rentals, Inc.
P.O. Box 1669
Annapolis, Maryland 21404

69

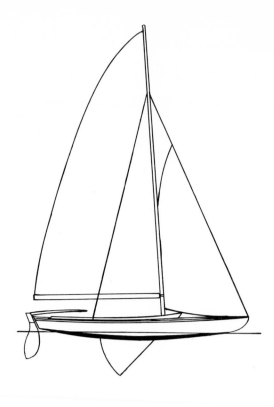

HAMPTON

Length overall 18′
Length at waterline 14′
Beam 5′9½″
Maximum draft 3′6″
Sail area 190 square feet
Weight 500 pounds

The Hampton is the largest one-design racing class on the Chesapeake Bay. She is a hard-chine V-bottom sloop available in either cedar-planked, plywood, or molded fiberglass construction. She is a lively, fast boat, sailed with a crew of one to four. No spinnaker is carried, but a trapeze is used when racing. Having a large cockpit, she is a good boat for day sailing. Kits are available for home finishing.

BOW Manufacturing
P.O. Box 279
Hampton, Virginia 23369

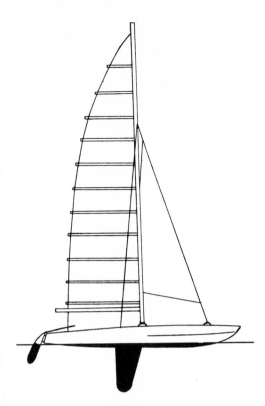

C

HELLCAT MARK III S

Length overall 25'
Beam 14'
Maximum draft 3'6"
Sail area 300 square feet

This big C class catamaran is affectionately called the "King of the Cats." The hulls are cold-molded plywood, and the beams and spars are aluminum. Cockpit is terylene reinforced with aluminum tubes. Like her smaller sister, the Hellcat, she folds in the center to a five-foot width for easy trailering. While she has a generous sail area, reefing is unnecessary in all but the severest conditions. She is perfectly safe, roomy, and easy to handle as a family boat, yet has the high performance so desirable for racing.

Alleman Enterprises
5819 South Shandle Drive
Mentor, Ohio 44060

HIGHLANDER

Length overall 20'
Beam 6'8"
Draft 4'10" centerboard down
Sail area 225 square feet
Weight 550 pounds

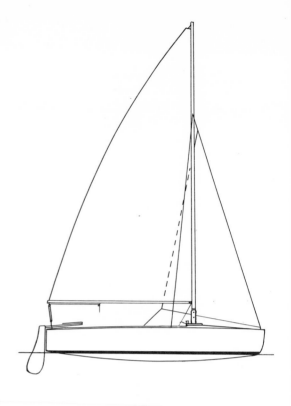

Designed for racing or family day sailing, the Highlander is a decked centerboarder available in fiberglass or molded plywood. She carries a spinnaker, and class rules permit a crew of three or four, but as a day sailer she has ample room for six or seven. Her hard bilges give good stability, and her flat after sections help her plane easily. Kits are available for the home builder. She can be trailered easily.

Douglass and McLeod, Inc.
P.O. Box 311
Painesville, Ohio 44077

INTERLAKE

Length overall 18'
Length at waterline 15'
Draft 4'8" centerboard down
Sail area 175 square feet
Weight 650 pounds

The Interlake is one of the oldest one-design class sailboats in America. Originally built of wood, she was converted to fiberglass in 1955. With her V-bottom and hard-chine, she has excellent stability, and the rocker to her keel adds to her weatherliness in steep seas. She is a good family day sailer, and safe for kids or beginners. She has built-in flotation and six hundred pounds of reserve buoyancy when full of water. The aluminum mast and boom are foam-filled. Most of the racing fleets are in the Midwest.

Customflex, Inc.
1817 Palmwood Avenue
Toledo, Ohio 43607

14

INTERNATIONAL 14

Length overall 14′
Beam 5′5″
Minimum weight 225 pounds
Maximum sail area 125 square feet

Strictly a development class, this world-famous planing dinghy has been radically improved through the years, and there are over two thousand registered, world-wide. Now available in fiberglass construction, she has acquired an impressive racing record in this hottest of all restricted open-class planing dinghies. She flies a spinnaker, and with her very light weight you can expect a very exciting performance in a breeze. She can be cartopped as well as trailered.

W. D. Schock Company
3502 South Greenville Street
Santa Ana, California 92704

JET 14

Length overall 14'
Beam 4'8"
Draft 4'2" centerboard down
Sail area 113 square feet
Weight 165 pounds

The Jet 14 is a high-performance, one-design racing sloop with a planing hull, now available in fiberglass. Lively and very fast, she is extremely sensitive to helm and weight changes. She is raced with a crew of two who must be mentally alert, with instant reflexes, to get the maximum performance. She carries a spinnaker, and the hull has flotation tanks. She can be cartopped, and is easily trailered. For the young racing skipper who wants to train for international competition, this is the boat.

Siddons and Sindle, Inc.
17 Central Avenue
Island Heights, New Jersey 08732

KITE

Length overall 11'7"
Beam 5'
Sail area 78 square feet
Weight 160 pounds

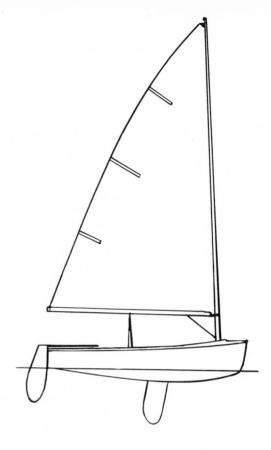

The Kite is a lively little sailing dinghy for family fun. Large enough to be sailed or raced by one or two adults, she can be handled easily by the youngsters. The fiberglass hull has foam flotation and is unsinkable. The flexible spruce mast, patterned after the Olympic Finn, is unstayed and can be quickly stepped and rigged. The boat can be cartopped as well as trailered. An excellent singlehander for the teenager.

Newport Boats
1919 Placentia
Costa Mesa, California 92627

LEADER

Length overall 14'
Length at waterline 13'
Beam 5'5"
Maximum draft 3'6"
Sail area 118 square feet
Weight 230 pounds

The Leader is a double-chine, plywood centerboard sloop, used for day sailing and racing in the Great Lakes area and Canada. A good fun boat for a couple of adults or youngsters. She carries a spinnaker, and is a smart sailer, easily handled. Kits are available for the home builder.

Croce and Lofthouse Sailcraft, Ltd.
4226 Kingston Road
Toronto, Ontario, Canada

LIDO 14

Length overall 14'
Beam 6'
Draft 4'3"
Sail area 111 square feet
Weight 300 pounds

The Lido 14 is a fiberglass sloop for family day sailing or racing. She has a molded deck and fore-and-aft seats, with built-in flotation. An ideal trainer or first boat for a youngster, she can carry up to six persons safely, and is a smart, lively sailer. She has anodized-aluminum spars and a loose-footed mainsail.

W. D. Schock Company
3502 South Greenville Street
Santa Ana, California 92704

LIGHTNING

Length overall 19′
Length at waterline 15′3″
Beam 6′6″
Draft 4′11″
Sail area 117 square feet; with spinnaker,
   300 square feet

One of the most popular of her size, this boat of the International Class has over ten thousand registered owners. Of V-bottom construction, she is available in either fiberglass or wood. She carries a spinnaker, and class rules specify a racing crew of three. With excellent stability, a large cockpit, and plenty of stowage space under the deck, she is a fine day sailer. She is very easy to handle, and can carry up to five people for relaxed sailing with safety.

Siddons and Sindle, Inc.
17 Central Avenue
Island Heights, New Jersey 08732

L16

LUDERS 16

Length overall 26′4″
Length at waterline 16′4″
Beam 5′9″
Draft 4′
Sail area 260 square feet
Displacement 2950 pounds

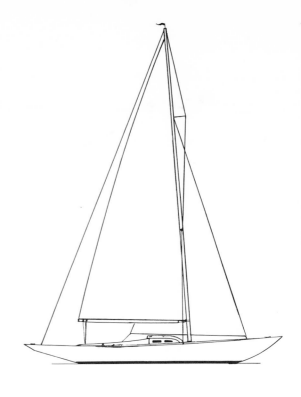

The classic L-16 is a racing yacht designed for International competition. Of molded fiberglass, with long overhangs, ballast keel, and minimum wetted surface, she is fast, close-winded, and very responsive to the helm. The cockpit has room for six, and there are two bunks below for overnight trips. Hardware and equipment are top quality. She can be trailered for interfleet competition.

Continental Plastics Corporation
2011 Placentia
Costa Mesa, California 92627

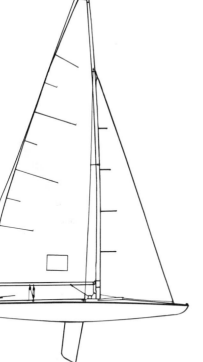

M-20

Length overall 20′
Length at waterline 16′
Beam 5′8″
Maximum draft 3′6″
Sail area: 167 square feet; with
spinnaker, 342 square feet

The M-20 is a molded fiberglass tunneled hull racing scow with twin bilgeboards. In the one-of-a-kind series she proved to be the fastest sailboat of her size, excluding catamarans. While there is a National class organization, the majority of the boats are raced in the Midwest. They carry a spinnaker, and race with a crew of two. With a large cockpit and deck, the M-20 is a good day sailer for four or five. She has built-in flotation, and is easily trailered.

Melges Boat Works, Inc.
Zenda, Wisconsin 53195

MERCURY

Length overall 18'
Length at waterline 13'
Beam 5'4"
Draft 3'1"
Sail area 277 square feet
Weight 1125 pounds

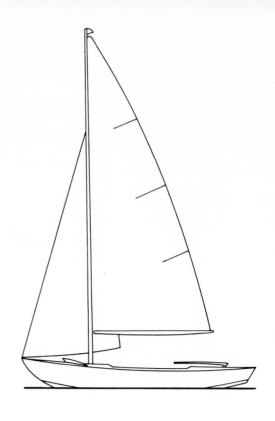

The Mercury is a hard-chine keel boat popular on the West Coast for racing and day
sailing. She is a smart sailer, easily handled, and very seaworthy in rough, choppy
waters. With 635 pounds of outside ballast,
she has excellent stability for relaxed sailing. While she is raced with a crew of two,
she can be day sailed comfortably with
four. Her hull is fiberglass and spars are
spruce.

W. D. Schock Company
3502 South Greenville Street
Santa Ana, California 92704

MOBJACK

Length overall 17′
Length at waterline 16′9″
Beam 6′6″
Sail area 180 square feet
Weight 460 pounds

This open-cockpit sloop is a versatile day sailer-racer, with a particular appeal for teenagers. The fiberglass hull is unsinkable, since it has a double bottom. With ample flare forward, she is a dry boat, ghosts easily in light airs, and moves fast under spinnaker. She has roller reefing boom for heavy weather. Strict class rules permit only one suit of sails, which keeps down costs of racing. Cockpit is self-bailing. Transom is reinforced to carry an outboard.

Newport Boats
1919 Placentia
Costa Mesa, California 92627

O. K. DINGHY

Length overall 13′1½″
Length at waterline 12′4″
Beam 4′7¾″
Sail area 90 square feet
Minimum weight 158½ pounds

This high-performance one-man planing dinghy offers exciting competition to the experienced racing enthusiast. The class has six hundred and thirty registered owners in the United States, and about six thousand world-wide. Her principal characteristics are a very light, compartmented hull, and an unstayed, bendy mast. Extremely lively and sensitive, she takes off on a plane at thrilling speeds. Construction is composite—plywood and fiberglass—and kits are available for the home builder. With her simple rig and light weight, she is easily cartopped.

Westin's Boat Shop
River Road
Sayville, New York 11782

110

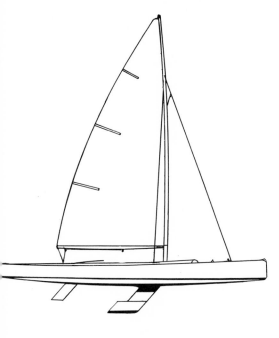

110
(INTERNATIONAL)

Length overall 24′
Length at waterline 18′
Beam 4′2″
Draft 2′9″
Sail area 167 square feet

The 110 is a keel sloop designed specifi-
cally for racing. Organized in 1939, the
International 110 class now numbers over
seven hundred. Double-enders with a flat
bottom and a 300-pound fin keel, the majority are of plywood construction, but class
rules now permit the use of fiberglass.
They have good initial stability, are close-
winded and smart sailers. Styrofoam blocks
are fitted for flotation, and the boat may be
sailed even when full of water. A trailer
can be had to transport the boat from port
to port.

Graves Yacht Yards
P.O. Box 36
Marblehead, Massachusetts 01945

P

PACIFIC CAT

Length overall 18′9″
Beam 7′11″
Draft 2′11″ centerboard down
Sail area 267 square feet
Weight 540 pounds

The Pacific Catamaran is one of the fastest one-design boats in the country. It has been clocked at better than twenty knots. The class organization has fleets on both coasts and in Hawaii. The spars are aluminum and the mainsail has full-length battens. One excellent feature is a roller luff-spar, which permits the jib to be reefed under way. The fiberglass hulls have foam flotation, and kick-up rudders for easy beaching.

Newport Boats
1919 Placentia
Costa Mesa, California 92627

PENGUIN

Length overall 11'6"
Length at waterline 11'2"
Beam 4'6"
Sail area 72 square feet
Minimum weight 135 pounds

The International Penguin Class Dinghy Association now has over eight thousand registered owners in the United States and South America. Although the boat was originally designed for plywood construction, the class has approved fiberglass hulls and the two types now race on an even footing. In the New England area the Penguin is popular among some clubs for frostbiting. Being entirely open and light in weight, she is primarily suited for day sailing and racing in sheltered waters rather than heavy weather and rough seas. She is light enough to be cartopped.

McNair Marine, Inc.
Killingsworth Road
Route 81
Higganum, Connecticut 06441

RAINBOW

Length overall 24'2"
Length at waterline 17'3"
Beam 6'3"
Draft 3'6"
Sail area 278 square feet

The Rainbow is a fiberglass, fin-keel, racing day sailer. With a masthead rig and permanent backstay, this sloop has an 1120-pound fin keel for stiffness and high-performance sailing. She has aluminum spars, and carries a spinnaker. With a large, deep cockpit, she provides comfortable day sailing for most families. Under the cuddy cabin are two berths and a head, so the boat can be used for overnight or weekend cruising.

Ray Greene and Company, Inc.
508 South Byrne Road
Toledo, Ohio 43609

REBEL

Length overall 16′
Length at waterline 14′9″
Beam 6′6″
Draft 3′ centerboard down
Sail area 166 square feet
Weight 700 pounds

Now in her nineteenth year, the Rebel is an established racing class. Of molded fiberglass, she is an excellent family day sailer, able, weatherly, and easy to sail. She has foam flotation and self-bailing cockpit. She is available with three deck plans—the Standard has wide deck and open cockpit, the Mark II has a long cockpit and contoured seats, and the Mark III has a molded cuddy cabin. Spars are aluminum and centerboard is steel. The boat is easy to trail, and an outboard bracket can be fitted for auxiliary power.

Ray Greene and Company, Inc.
508 South Byrne Road
Toledo, Ohio 43609

-R-B-

RHODES BANTAM

Length overall 14′
Length at waterline 13′11″
Beam 5′6¼″
Draft: centerboard up, 5½″; centerboard down, 4′2″
Sail area 125 square feet
Weight 325 pounds

The Bantam is a hard-chine sloop of plywood or fiberglass construction, with aluminum spars. She is an excellent first boat, as a trainer or day sailer. She is easy to handle, roomy and stable. For racing, there is optional equipment, such as genoa jib and spinnaker, boom vangs, hiking straps, and tiller extension. Fiberglass hull and parts kits, and prefab mahogany plywood kits are available. Organized in 1946, the class numbers over fifteen hundred world-wide.

Customflex, Inc.
1817 Palmwood
Toledo, Ohio 43607

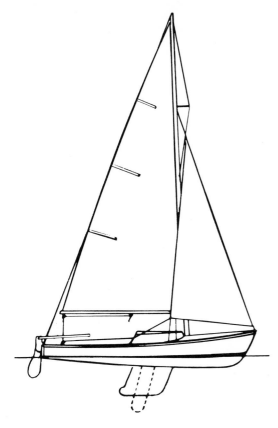

ROHDES 19

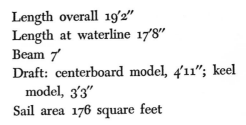

Length overall 19′2″
Length at waterline 17′8″
Beam 7′
Draft: centerboard model, 4′11″; keel
    model, 3′3″
Sail area 176 square feet

With more than thirty racing fleets, the Rhodes 19 class is one of the largest in the United States. Of fiberglass construction, she is available as a centerboarder for shoal waters, or with a 415-pound keel for blue-water racing. As a day sailer, she has a roomy cockpit for six or seven, and a shelter cabin for overnight trips. Forward deck is ample for spinnaker handling. She has a well in afterdeck for an outboard motor.

The O'Day Company
168 Stevens Street
Fall River, Massachusetts 02722

SHARK ONE-DESIGN AND B CLASS

Length overall 20'
Length at waterline 18'7"
Beam 10'
Sail area 272 square feet
Weight 350 pounds

Shark is the largest one-design catamaran class, and the fastest, with over two hundred and ninety registered in the United States and Canada. Built of fiberglass and aluminum, she is dry, responsive, and very maneuverable. One of her outstanding features is her portability. After the removal of only one bolt, she can be folded to a width of five feet for easy trailering. She has tilting centerboards and four storage compartments. For family fun she is safe and a real thrill to sail.

Alleman Enterprises
5819 South Shandle Drive
Mentor, Ohio 44060

942-3100

SHIELDS ONE-DESIGN

Length overall 30'2½"
Length at waterline 20'
Beam 6'5¼"
Draft 4'9"
Sail area 498 square feet
Displacement 4600 pounds

This fiberglass keel racing sloop offers the ultimate in one-design competition for the experienced skipper. Her fine lines and long overhangs result in a lively, well-balanced boat that is fast in light weather or a hard breeze. The hull incorporates flotation compartments and watertight bulkheads. Fleets of these boats are in use at the U. S. Naval Academy and the Merchant Marine Academy and Shields has been chosen for numerous intercollegiate competitions.

Chris-Craft Corporation
P.O. Box 860
Pompano Beach, Florida 33061

SKIPJACK

Length overall 14′7″
Beam 5′3″
Sail area 125 square feet
Weight 320 pounds

A high-performance sailing dinghy, the Skipjack is used at the U. S. Naval Academy for its sailing programs. Fiberglass hull and aluminum mast have foam flotation, making her unsinkable. Mainsail has full-length battens. The rounded deck-edges make hiking comfortable, and the cockpit floor is above the waterline, making her self-bailing. She planes quickly, points high, and foots fast. She has enough stability to be used for day sailing or junior training.

Newport Boats
1919 Placentia
Costa Mesa, California 92627

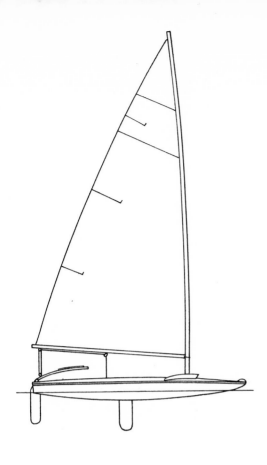

SKYLARK

Length overall 14′2″
Beam 4′8″
Sail area 100 square feet
Weight 260 pounds

The Skylark is a one-design sailing class with a fiberglass tunnel planing hull, having some of the characteristics of a sailing board and a catamaran. She has an unstayed bending aluminum mast and aluminum bilge boards. She has a shallow cockpit for legroom, and can carry three persons. Skylark planes easily, and is exciting to sail or race. She is unsinkable, has excellent initial stability, and can be cartopped.

Starcraft Corporation
P.O. Box 577
Goshen, Indiana 46526

SNIPE

Length overall 15'6"
Length at waterline 13'6"
Beam 4'8"
Sail area 128 square feet
Weight 425 pounds minimum

The most popular small sailboat racing class in the world, the International Snipe Class has over eighteen thousand boats in 503 fleets in twenty-eight countries. Originally she was built of wood to rigid one-design specifications, but class rules now approve fiberglass construction. The Snipe is considered tops as a day sailer and racer for youngsters and the young-at-heart. She is fast, exciting to sail, sensitive to the helm, and performs beautifully under all conditions.

W. D. Schock Company
3502 South Greenville Street
Santa Ana, California 92704

Length overall 9′4″
Beam 4′5″
Sail area 67 square feet
Weight 125 pounds, less equipment

The Boston Whaler Squall is a versatile dinghy of double fiberglass, urethane foam filled, and therefore unsinkable. As a smart, able sailing dinghy she is ideal for the novice as well as the experienced. As a yacht tender she may be rowed from two positions, carry four persons comfortably, and may be powered by an outboard up to 3 hp. The lateen sail has aluminum spars designed to float, and the centerboard is lever-operated and cannot be lost in the event of a capsizal. She has a padlocked locker in the seat aft to stow your lunch or loose gear.

The Fisher-Pierce Company, Inc.
1149 Hingham Street
Rockland, Massachusetts 02370

STAR

Length overall 22'8"
Length at waterline 15'6"
Beam 5'8"
Draft 3'4"
Sail area 285 square feet
Keel weight 900 pounds

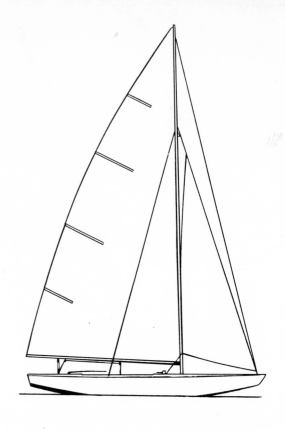

With over five thousand boats registered in the International Class, the world-famous Star offers the highest type of competition for the man who takes his racing seriously. Now in her fifty-eighth year, this two-man keel boat has been improved and highly engineered to maximum performance. Class rules now allow fiberglass hulls as an alternative to the conventional wood. Stars carry no spinnakers, and as an economy measure you are allowed to buy but one suit of sails a year. The boats are commonly trailered about the country for maximum participation in important series.

Old Greenwich Boat Company
180 Southfield Avenue
Stamford, Connecticut 06902

THISTLE

Length overall 17′
Beam 6′
Draft 4′6″ centerboard down
Sail area 175 square feet
Weight 300 pounds

With over twenty-five hundred owners, in one hundred and twenty-five fleets, the Thistle is one of the best-known racing boats. Built of molded plywood or fiberglass, she is fast and lively, and planes even in light winds. Though the boat is raced with a crew of two or three, the cockpit seats five comfortably as a day sailer, and the flared bow sections keep the boat dry. The cockpit is deep, and you sit down inside on seats with the coaming as a backrest. Building kits are available in various stages of completion. With her light weight and high performance, the Thistle is truly an exciting boat to sail or race.

Douglass and McLeod, Inc.
P.O. Box 311
Painesville, Ohio 44077

TOWN CLASS

Length overall 16'6"
Beam 5'9"
Sail area 152 square feet
Weight 600 pounds

For over thirty years the Town Class has been a popular one-design racing class in clubs along the Atlantic Coast. Now available in fiberglass, this is an able, wholesome design suitable for rough waters and heavy winds. With a 55-pound metal centerboard and a sail plan with a low center of effort, the boat is stiff on her feet and safe for kids or family sailing.

Town Class Boats
Lane's End
Newbury, Massachusetts 01950

210

210
(INTERNATIONAL)

Length overall 29'10"
Length at waterline 24'
Beam 5'10"
Draft 3'10"
Sail area 305 square feet
Displacement 2400 pounds
Ballast 1175 pounds

Organized as a class in 1946, the 210 now has sixteen fleets in the United States and Hawaii. Often called the 110's big sister, the 210 is also a double-ended keel sloop of plywood construction, bronze fastened over oak frames. Styrofoam flotation is provided. The 210 is a sharp sailer, sensitive and responsive to the helm, and provides the highest type of competition.

Graves Yacht Yards
P.O. Box 36
Marblehead, Massachusetts 01945

U. S. MONOTYPE

Length overall 14′2″
Beam 5′8″
Sail area 95 square feet
Weight 240 pounds

The Monotype is a cat-rigged single-hander, a racing boat of high performance for Olympics-like sailing. With weights cut to a minimum, she sails fast, points high, and readily planes in the lightest airs. She has a dagger board, and a portable 25-pound lead ballast to be moved from side to side. Her one-of-a-kind rating is 11.8. Frame kits are available for plywood hulls, and there is a fiberglass version. Spars are spruce.

Ellie's Boat Works
1300 North Betty Lane
Clearwater, Florida 33515

WAYFARER

Length overall 15'10"
Length at waterline 14'10"
Beam 6'1"
Maximum draft 3'10"
Sail area 141 square feet
Weight 365 pounds

Popular in the Midwest and Canada, the Wayfarer is a double-chine, centerboard sloop of plywood or fiberglass construction. She is used as a day sailer, camper, or racer. Lively and fast, she is sensitive to sail and planes easily. Excellent for junior training, and is easy to trail and launch.

Avon Sailboats
1033 East Auburn Road
Rochester, Michigan 48063

WINDMILL

Length overall 15'6"
Beam 4'8"
Draft 4'2", centerboard down
Sail area 119 square feet
Weight 198 pounds

The Windmill is a high-performance one-design racing sloop that has achieved great popularity in recent years, both here and abroad. There are over two thousand registered in the United States, and fleets as far away as Finland. Inexpensive, light in weight, and very fast, she offers exciting competition to the most ardent skipper. Relatively narrow of beam, she might be called an open-cockpit boat, with full-length washboards in lieu of decks. Formerly built of plywood, the Windmill Class has now approved of fiberglass construction.

Durabilt Corporation
Murray Road
Winston-Salem, North Carolina 27106

OTHER RACING BOATS—CENTERBOARD CLASSES

BEETLE CAT
12'4"×6'×2'6". Sail area 100 square feet. Gaff-rigged. Wood hull and spars. Races with crew of two.

Concordia Company, Inc.
South Wharf
South Dartmouth, Massachusetts 02748

COMET
16'×5'×3'6". Sail area 130 square feet. Fiberglass or wood hull, aluminum or wood spars. Positive buoyancy. Races with crew of two.

Siddons and Sindle, Inc.
17 Central Avenue
Island Heights, New Jersey 08732

C LARK
14'×5'9"×3'6". Sail area 131 square feet, plus spinnaker. Fiberglass hull, aluminum spars. Buoyancy: self-rescuing. Race with crew of two.

Clark Boat Company
18817 East Valley Highway
Kent, Washington 98031

DEMON
15'×5'3"×3'2". Sail area 116 square feet, plus spinnaker. Fiberglass hull, aluminum spars. Buoyancy: self-rescuing. Race with crew of two.

Advance Sailboat Corporation
16400 East Truman Road
Independence, Missouri 64050

C SCOW
20'×6'8"×3'6". Sail area 216 square feet. Cat rig. Buoyancy: self-rescuing. Wood or fiberglass hull, wood spars. Twin bilgeboards. Races with crew of two.

Melges Boat Works, Inc.
Zenda, Wisconsin 53195

DYER DELTA
18'8"×6'1"×4'6". Sail area 189 square feet, plus spinnaker. Fiberglass hull, aluminum spars. Positive flotation. Races with crew of three.

The Anchorage
57 Miller Street
Warren, Rhode Island 02885

CAPE DORY 14
14'6"×4'3"×3'6". Sail area 85 square feet. Cat rig. Weight 250 pounds. Fiberglass hull, aluminum spars. Races with crew of one.

Cape Dory Company
373 Crescent Street
West Bridgewater, Massachusetts 02379

E SCOW
28'×6'9"×4'9". Sail area 319 square feet, plus spinnaker. Wood or fiberglass hull, wood spars. Buoyancy: self-rescuing. Races with crew of three. Has twin bilgeboards.

Melges Boat Works, Inc.
Zenda, Wisconsin 53195

EXPLORER

17'×6'4"×4'6". Sail area 147 square feet, plus spinnaker. Fiberglass hull, aluminum spars. Positive flotation. Races with crew of two or three.

Sailstar Boats, Inc.
1 Constitution Street
Bristol, Rhode Island 02809

FALCON

15'8"×5'9"×2'10". Sail area 137 square feet, plus spinnaker. Fiberglass hull, aluminum spars. Positive flotation. Races with crew of two.

Sterling Boatbuilding Corporation
P.O. Box 106
East Greenwich, Rhode Island 02818

FIREBALL

16'2"×4'8½"×4'½". Sail area 123 square feet, plus spinnaker. Wood or fiberglass hull. Positive flotation. Races with crew of two.

Westin's Boat Shop
River Road
Sayville, New York 11782

5-0-5

16'6"×6'6"×3'9". Sail area 172 square feet, no spinnaker. Fiberglass or wood hull, aluminum or wood spars. Built-in flotation. Races with crew of two. Trapeze employed.

Royal Sailboats Company
1815 Northwest Boulevard
Columbus, Ohio 43221

420

13'9"×5'5"×3'2". Sail area 110 square feet, plus spinnaker. Fiberglass hull, wood or aluminum spars. Positive flotation. Buoyancy: self-rescuing. Races with crew of two. Trapeze employed.

Nautica Corporation
P.O. Box 26
Paramus, New Jersey 07652

G.P. 14

14'×5'×3'7". Sail area 102 square feet, no spinnaker. Wood hull, wood spars. Positive flotation. Races with crew of two.

John Wright, Jr.
328 West Queen Lane
Philadelphia, Pennsylvania 19144

GEARY 18

18'×5'2"×4'8". Sail area 157 square feet, no spinnaker. Wood or fiberglass hull, wood or aluminum spars. Buoyancy: self-rescuing. Races with crew of two.

Clark Boat Company
18817 East Valley Highway
Kent, Washington 98031

INTERCLUB

11'6"×4'7"×3'5". Sail area 72 square feet. Cat rig. Fiberglass hull, aluminum spars. Positive flotation. Races with crew of two.

The O'Day Corporation
168 Stevens Street
Fall River, Massachusetts 02722

KOHINOOR

15'3"×6'×4'9". Sail area 145 square feet, no spinnaker. Wood hull, wood spars. Buoyancy: none added. Races with crew of two.

Wright-built Boat Company
Dundee, New York 14837

LONE STAR 13

13'×5'×3'. Sail area 93 square feet, no spinnaker. Masthead rig. Fiberglass hull, aluminum spars. Has twin bilgeboards, built-in flotation. Races with crew of two.

Chrysler Boat Corporation
1001 Industrial Avenue
Plano, Texas 75074

LONE STAR 16

16'×6'1"×3'10". Sail area 160 square feet, plus spinnaker. Fiberglass hull, aluminum spars. Positive flotation. Has twin bilgeboards. Races with crew of three.

> Chrysler Boat Corporation
> 1001 Industrial Avenue
> Plano, Texas 75074

M SCOW

16'×5'8"×2'8". Sail area 146 square feet, no spinnaker. Wood or fiberglass hull, wood spars. Twin bilgeboards. Buoyancy: self-rescuing. Races with crew of two.

> Melges Boat Works, Inc.
> Zenda, Wisconsin 53195

M-16

16'×5'6"×2'6". Sail area 150 square feet, no spinnaker. Wood or fiberglass hull, wood spars. Buoyancy: self-rescuing. Bilgeboard scow. Races with crew of two.

> Melges Boat Works, Inc.
> Zenda, Wisconsin 53195

MIRROR DINGHY

10'10"×4'7"×2'9". Sail area 69 square feet, no spinnaker. Sloop rig. Wood hull, wood spars. Buoyancy: self-rescuing. Races with crew of two.

> James Bliss and Company
> Route 128
> Dedham, Massachusetts 02026

MOTH

11'×4'9"×3'. Sail area 82 square feet. Cat rig. Buoyancy: optional. Fiberglass hull, wood or aluminum spars. Races with crew of one.

> Royal Sailboats Company
> 1815 Northwest Boulevard
> Columbus, Ohio 43221

NATIONAL ONE-DESIGN

17'×5'8"×3'6". Sail area 137 square feet, no spinnaker. Wood or fiberglass hull, wood or aluminum spars. Buoyancy: self-rescuing. Races with crew of two.

> Fiberglass Unlimited
> 8133 Milmont Street
> Massilon, Ohio 44646

NIPPER

12'×5'2"×2'8". Sail area 100 square feet, no spinnaker. Cat rig. Wood or fiberglass hull, wood or aluminum spars. Buoyancy: none added. Races with crew of two.

> Ray Greene and Company
> 508 South Byrne Road
> Toledo, Ohio 43609

OMEGA

13'7"×5'4"×3'. Sail area 108 square feet, no spinnaker. Fiberglass hull, aluminum spars. Positive flotation. Races with crew of two.

> Wesco Marine
> 8211 Lankershim Boulevard
> North Hollywood, California 91605

OPTIMIST PRAM

8'×4'×2'6". Sail area 35 square feet. Positive flotation. Wood hull, wood spars. Races with crew of one or two.

> Ellie's Boat Works, Inc.
> 1300 North Betty Lane
> Clearwater, Florida 33515

RAVEN

24'2"×7'×5'4". Sail area 300 square feet, plus spinnaker. Wood or fiberglass hull, aluminum spars. Buoyancy: positive flotation. Races with crew of three.

> Cape Cod Shipbuilding Company
> Narrows Road
> Wareham, Massachusetts 02571

SPARKLER

11′×4′6″×2′6″. Sail area 70 square feet, no spinnaker. Buoyancy: self-rescuing. Fiberglass hull, aluminum spars. Races with crew of one.

Ellie's Boat Works
1300 North Betty Lane
Clearwater, Florida 33515

STARFISH

13′8″×4′×2′4″. Sail area 82 square feet. Lateen rig. Positive flotation. Fiberglass hull, aluminum spars. Races with crew of one.

Fillip Manufacturing Company
1923 Austin Street
San Angelo, Texas 76901

SUPER SATELLITE

14′×6′×3′6″. Sail area 130 square feet, no spinnaker. Fiberglass hull, aluminum spars. Positive flotation. Race with crew of two.

Wesco Marine
8211 Lankershim Boulevard
North Hollywood, California 91605

WINDJAMMER

16′9″×6′6″×4′7″. Sail area 158 square feet, no spinnaker. Fiberglass hull, aluminum spars. Buoyancy: self-rescuing. Races with crew of two.

Chesapeake Marine Industries, Inc.
13193 Warwick Boulevard
Newport News, Virginia 23607

Y-FLYER

18′×5′8″×4′. Sail area 161 square feet, no spinnaker. Buoyancy: self-rescuing. Plywood or fiberglass hull, wood or aluminum spars. Races with crew of two.

Glenn Mottin Sailboat Sales and
Manufacturing Company
8005 Monroe, St. Louis, Missouri 63114

COLUMBIA 5.5
32'5"×6'3"×4'4". Sail area 311 square feet, plus spinnaker. Fiberglass hull, aluminum spars. Flotation tanks. Races with crew of three.

> Columbia Yacht Corporation
> 275 McCormick Avenue
> Costa Mesa, California 92626

COLUMBIA 21
21'8"×7'7"×3'3". Sail area 234 square feet, plus spinnaker. Fiberglass hull, aluminum spars. Races with crew of two.

> Columbia Yacht Corporation
> 275 McCormick Avenue
> Costa Mesa, California 92626

CRESCENT
24'×7'×4'1". Sail area 298 square feet, plus spinnaker. Fiberglass hull, aluminum spars. Racing crew of three.

> Customflex, Inc.
> 1817 Palmwood Avenue
> Toledo, Ohio 43607

ORION
19'×6'9"×4'6" (centerboard version available, 1'8" draft). Sail area 200 square feet. Fiberglass hull, aluminum spars. Has positive flotation. Races with crew of two.

> Sailstar Boats, Inc.
> 1 Constitution Avenue
> Bristol, Rhode Island 02809

SCHOCK 25
25'×7'×4'. Sail area 222 square feet, plus spinnaker. Fiberglass hull, aluminum spars. Buoyancy: self-rescuing. Races with crew of three.

> W. D. Schock Company
> 3502 South Greenville Street
> Santa Ana, California 92704

OTHER RACING BOATS—MULTIHULL CLASSES

A-LION
18′×7′6″×2′6″. Sail area 150 square feet, no spinnaker. Cat rig. Fiberglass hull, aluminum spars. Positive flotation. Raced singlehanded.

> American Fiberglass Corporation
> Rockland Road
> Norwalk, Connecticut 06856

TIGER CAT
17′×7′11½″×3′1″. Sail area 180 square feet, no spinnaker. Fiberglass hull, aluminum spars. Positive flotation. Races with crew of two.

> Lippincott Boat Works
> Canal Avenue
> Riverton, New Jersey 08077

COUGAR MKIII
18′9″×7′11½″×2′8″. Sail area 235 square feet, no spinnaker. Fiberglass hull, aluminum spars. Positive flotation. Races with crew of two.

> Rebcats
> 733 Fifteenth Street N.W.
> Washington, D.C. 20016

TORNADO
20′×10′×2′6″. Sail area 235 square feet, no spinnaker. Wood hull, fiberglassed. Aluminum spars. Buoyancy: self-rescuing. Races with crew of two. Employs trapeze.

> Alleman Enterprises
> 5819 South Shandle Drive
> Mentor, Ohio 44060

PHOENIX
18′×7′11″×2′8″. Sail area 220 square feet, no spinnaker. Fiberglass hull, aluminum spars. Employs trapeze. Positive flotation. Races with crew of two.

> Gibbs Boat Company
> LaSalle, Michigan 48145

TRIUMPH 24
Trimaran—24′×14′×3′. Sail area 242 square feet, no spinnaker. Fiberglass hulls, aluminum spars. Positive flotation. Races with crew of two.

> Lasco Marine
> Hope Street
> Alviso, California 95002

SHEARWATER
16′6″×7′6″×5′. Sail area 235 square feet, no spinnaker. Fiberglass hull, aluminum spars. Employs trapeze. Positive flotation. Races with crew of two.

> McNichols Boat Sales
> 1617 East McNichols Street
> Detroit, Michigan 48203

6 Cruising Auxiliaries

It has often been said that every boat is a compromise—that for every desirable feature you may have to sacrifice another equally desirable.

Nowhere is this more true than in buying a small cruising sailboat. Boatbuilders are well aware of this, and by their efforts the buyers' problems have been simplified to a considerable degree. In recent years there has been a notable increase in the production of small cruising sailers, twenty-four feet and under. The ingenuity and creative thinking that have gone into their design, to offer maximum accommodations in the minimum space, are commendable.

The majority of these boats are of shoal draft, for maximum utility. Some are centerboarders, others have a keel and centerboard. Twin bilge keels are gaining in popularity, since they combine shoal draft with the sailing characteristics of the true keel boat. Many of these (and larger) boats are powered by an outboard, fitted in a well in the afterdeck. Thus the space normally required for an inboard engine is added to the living area.

There is one feature about outboard motors for auxiliary power that some boat owners find objectionable. While the motor is running, the hatch over the motor well must be kept open, otherwise the motor would be starved for air. When the boat is running dead before the wind, exhaust fumes and motor noise will fill the cockpit, making it unpleasant for the occupants.

But the majority of owners feel that this occasional annoyance is more than compensated for by the additional living space

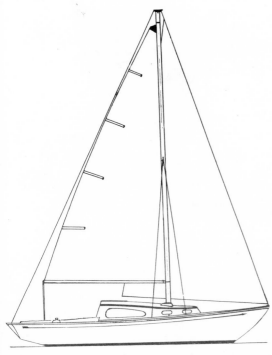

Acadian, sloop-rigged

gained. In the smaller cruising sailboat, every cubic inch of space in the living area must be used to its best advantage, and the installation of an inboard motor and all its accessories could result in a cramped, inconvenient galley, for example. As stated before, you just can't expect to get everything in a small boat.

The two features hardest to find in a small, shoal-draft sailboat are headroom and privacy. Full headroom is not an absolute necessity, for when you are below deck you'll normally be sitting. An enclosed toilet is most desirable, but if that cannot be arranged, a bulkhead with a sliding door or curtain gives some privacy where it is most appreciated.

Any experienced cruising man will assure you that a cockpit awning is an absolute must. Rigged over the boom with a couple of battens, and with side curtains to snap into place in inclement weather, it provides additional living space. When you are anchored on a hot day, it provides welcome relief from the broiling sun. On a rainy day you can be out in the open enjoying the sights, instead of cooped up below in cramped quarters feeling sorry for yourself. On a hot, oppressive night you can sleep in the cockpit, and this has a particular appeal to youngsters. When you get under way, it takes but a minute to roll it up and lash it on the cabin top.

A bow pulpit and lifelines should be given serious consideration. They are particularly important for the small cruising sailboat, where deck space is limited. They provide a safety factor when you are handling sails in heavy weather, and they are doubly important if children are aboard. While not all boats come equipped with them, they can easily be installed as a very worthwhile extra.

The most important instrument in promoting the small cruising sailboats is the Midget Ocean Racing Club (MORC). It was organized to sponsor safe medium-to-long-distance ocean racing on a handicap basis, in craft under thirty feet in length. Its rules, which lay down strict standards for seaworthiness and safety, have had a

healthy influence on small-boat design. Where cruising races were formerly limited to those owning the larger yachts, the MORC has brought the sport within reach of thousands of little fellows.

As you move up to the larger craft, you achieve more living comfort and convenience. With increased usable space, the designer has more latitude, and the accommodation plan is determined by choice rather than necessity. You can be assured of full headroom and more privacy. The enclosed head will have room for a shower. The galley will be more convenient, with plenty of elbow room and adequate counter space. Separate cabins insure maximum privacy, and there will be generous stowage room for sails, ship's gear, and everyone's belongings.

One builder offers as many as six different interior layouts for each of his models. The accommodations will be tailored to fit your specific requirements and decorated to suit your tastes. This is the nearest approach to a custom-built yacht that you can get in a production model.

One important advantage you achieve in the larger cruising auxiliary is the expanded cruising range. Greater fuel and water capacity, plus mechanical refrigeration, enables you to make more extended cruises. This is very important when you are cruising in waters where facilities for replenishing supplies are few and far between.

While the incidence of damage by lightning is infrequent, the possibility does exist, particularly since most yachts have aluminum spars. The best insurance against this is to be sure that the boat of your choice has the mast and rigging grounded to the keel.

Cruising auxiliary sailboats, since they are not strictly one-design, are raced with handicaps, individually applied. The boat's handicap, or rating, is arrived at by a formula of measurements. By means of tables in the North American Yacht Racing Union handbook, this rating is translated into *seconds per mile*, which is applied to the yacht's elapsed time.

There are two classifications in common use—the CCA (Cruising Club of America), and the MORC (Midget Ocean Racing Club) for boats under thirty feet.

Where ratings are given in this book, they are the *manufacturer's estimated* *rating*. Since the buyer has a choice of optional equipment, the boat's weight and measurements will vary individually. Therefore it is the owner's responsibility to obtain his own measurement certificate and rating.

ACADIAN ·

Length overall 30'
Length at waterline 21'
Beam 8'6"
Draft 4'4"
Sail area: sloop, 378 square feet;
   yawl, 394.5 square feet

As a sloop or yawl, the Acadian is a rugged family cruiser and offshore sailer. With a 3200-pound lead keel, she is powerful and able. Below, there are three berths, and a dinette converts to a fourth. Complete galley is aft. Toilet is fully enclosed, and mahogany doors insure privacy fore and aft. There is full headroom and plenty of storage space. Auxiliary power is a Universal Atomic Four. The cockpit is roomy and comfortable. The yawl steers with a wheel and the sloop with a tiller.

Paceship, Division of
Industrial Shipping Company, Ltd.
Mahone Bay, Nova Scotia, Canada

A Y

ALACRITY

Length overall 18'6"
Length at waterline 17'
Beam 6'11"
Draft 2'
Sail area 150 square feet
Weight 1450 pounds
CCA rating 16.5
MORC rating 14

The Alacrity is a true midget ocean racing sloop with twin bilge keels, each incorporating 240 pounds of ballast. If capsized, the boat is self-righting, in accordance with MORC rules. Accommodations are minimal in a boat of this size, but she has three berths, a toilet, space for a stove, and lockers. The bilge keels allow very shoal draft, yet give stability and dampen the roll when sailing before the wind. Spars are aluminum, with roller reefing. Outboard may be carried on stern bracket.

Wells Yachts, Inc.
50 Gregory Street
Marblehead, Massachusetts 01945

A30

ALBERG 30

Length overall 30′3″
Length at waterline 21′8″
Beam 8′9″
Draft 4′6″
Sail area 410 square feet
Displacement 9000 pounds
CCA rating 23.2

This modern auxiliary cruiser is an excellent choice for the skipper who wants a boat he can race but which also offers cruising accommodations normally found in larger craft. With a ballast keel of 3300 pounds, a masthead rig, and sleek lines, the Alberg 30 is fast, weatherly, and comfortable. She sleeps four in two separate cabins, has an enclosed head, and a commodious galley with 6′3″ headroom. She is powered with a 30-hp Atomic Four. Her hull is one-piece fiberglass laminate. Altogether, this is one of the best designs of her size.

Whitby Boat Works, Ltd.
570 Finley Avenue
Ajax, Ontario, Canada

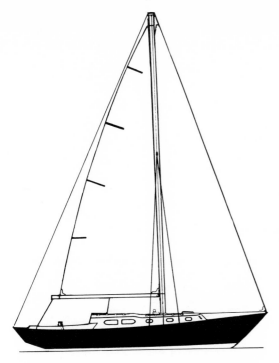

APACHE 37

Length overall 37'
Length at waterline 26'3"
Beam 10'2½"
Draft 5'9"
Sail area 606 square feet
Displacement 14,280 pounds
CCA rating 30.7

The Apache 37 is a fast offshore racing auxiliary with luxurious cruising accommodations for six. The light-displacement hull has a fin keel and blade rudder for minimum resistance. With a high aspect ratio and masthead rig, she is fast, weatherly, and very close-winded. The cabin is very roomy, with a dinette and spacious galley amidships. Toilet room has full headroom, and a shower is optional. Power is 30-hp Atomic Four.

Chris-Craft Corporation
P.O. Box 860
Pompano Beach, Florida 33061

ARIEL

Length overall 25'7"
Length at waterline 18'6"
Beam 8'
Draft 3'8"
Sail area 311 square feet
Displacement 5500 pounds
MORC rating 20.5

In terms of comfort and performance, the Ariel is a big boat for her size. With 2500 pounds of lead ballast in her keel and a masthead rig, she is stiff, able, and fast. The cockpit can seat six comfortably. The main cabin has 5'11" headroom, with two full-size berths, and an efficient galley aft. The forward cabin has two berths and a toilet, separated from the main cabin by lockers and a dresser. Interior trim is teak and formica. Auxiliary power is an outboard in a well aft, but inboard power, an Atomic Four, is optional and preferable. Spars are aluminum, with roller reefing.

Pearson Yachts
West Shore Road
Portsmouth, Rhode Island 02871

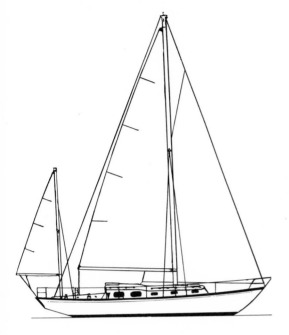

BLACK WATCH

Length overall 37′
Length at waterline 25′6″
Beam 10′6″
Draft 5′1″
Sail area 653 square feet
Displacement 17,500
CCA rating 28.5

This fiberglass auxiliary was designed for offshore cruising and racing, and may be sloop- or yawl-rigged. The cabin trunk and exterior trim is mahogany, and the interior is finished in teak. With an unusually roomy layout below, she sleeps seven in three cabins. The large galley has ample counter area, and the midships head has a stall shower. There is a chart table and navigator's station aft. Auxiliary power is a 31-hp Gray, and fuel and water tanks of ample capacity are in the keel.

Douglass and McLeod, Inc.
P.O. Box 311
Painesville, Ohio 44077

BLUE CHIP
(CAPE COD)

Length overall 29′10″
Length at waterline 23′2″
Beam 9′6″
Draft 4′3″
Sail area 465 square feet
Ballast keel 3250 pounds

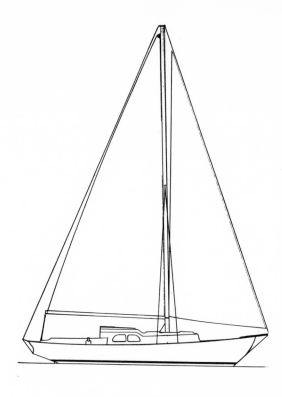

The fiberglass Blue Chip was designed for family cruising and racing under the MORC rules. With a masthead rig, large foretriangle, and long lateral plane, she sails with a lot of power and drive, yet is stiff enough for sailing comfort. The custom-built interior has four berths in two cabins, separated by toilet room and hanging locker. Galley and icebox are aft. Forward cabin has headroom in the dressing area. The comfortable cockpit is self-bailing and has a teak floor. Auxiliary power is a four-cylinder Palmer, sealed off from the cabin by a removable panel.

Cape Cod Shipbuilding Company
Narrows Road
Wareham, Massachusetts 02571

CALIFORNIA 20

Length overall 20′
Length at waterline 18′
Beam 7′
Draft 3′4″
Sail area 196 square feet
Displacement 1950 pounds

The Cal 20 is a salty, all-purpose family boat, for day sailing, cruising, or MORC racing. Over a thousand are in use on both coasts, the Great Lakes, and Hawaii, and there is a strong one-design class organization. The fiberglass hull has a fin keel, and she is self-righting. The raised deck design makes her a dry sailer and gives maximum room in the cabin. There are four berths in the two-compartment cabin, with space for lockers, toilet, and galley. The eight-foot-long cockpit is large enough for six when day sailing, and there is a well for outboard power. The aluminum mast has a hinged mast-step for convenience when trailering.

Jensen Marine Corporation
235 Fischer Street
Costa Mesa, California 92626

CALIFORNIA 25

Length overall 25'
Length at waterline 20'
Beam 8'
Draft 4'
Sail area 286 square feet
Displacement 4000 pounds
MORC rating 19.9
CCA rating 22.6

This all-fiberglass sloop is a combination of ocean racer and family cruiser. With a 1700-pound ballast keel and spade rudder, she is stiff, able, and weatherly. The cabin has four berths, and the wide convertible hatch cover can be raised and covered with a canvas dodger to provide full headroom with shelter. The forward compartment with enclosed head is separated from the main cabin by a bulkhead for privacy, and has a double berth. Main cabin features a dinette which converts to a double berth, a hanging locker, and galley. The transom has a removable section for mounting an outboard motor.

Jensen Marine Corporation
235 Fischer Street
Costa Mesa, California 92626

CALIFORNIA 34

Length overall 33'3"
Length at waterline 26'
Beam 10'
Draft 5'
Sail area 515 square feet
Displacement 9500 pounds
Ballast 3750 pounds
CCA rating 29.5

The Cal 34 is a high-performance cruiser/racer with a fin keel and spade rudder—long on the waterline, hard bilges, and light displacement. With a masthead rig and large foretriangle, the shrouds are led inboard to permit closer trimming of the headsails. The main cabin has a dinette and double berth, with full-length galley opposite. The forward cabin has a double berth with dresser and lockers. The head is separated from both cabins by two doors. Two quarter berths aft. Power is 30-hp Atomic Four with 2:1 reduction, which gives seven-knot speed. This is a fine craft for extended family cruises, able and comfortable for offshore sailing.

Jensen Marine Corporation
235 Fischer Street
Costa Mesa, California 92626

CALIFORNIA 40

Length overall 39'4"
Length at waterline 30'4"
Beam 11'
Draft 5'7"
Sail area 700 square feet
Displacement 15,000 pounds
CCA rating 36.1

The Cal 40 has piled up an enviable record in ocean racing, having won in the TRANSPAC, SORC, and Bermuda races. With long sleek lines, short keel, and masthead rig, she is a powerful sailer. There are berths for eight—two in the owner's cabin forward, four in the main cabin, and two quarter berths.

Jensen Marine Corporation
235 Fischer Street
Costa Mesa, California 92626

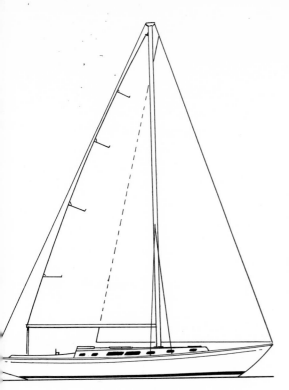

CALIFORNIA 48

Length overall 47'9"
Length at waterline 35'
Beam 12'
Draft 6'6"
Sail area 1040 square feet
Displacement 25,000 pounds
CCA rating 43.2

The Cal 48 is an outstanding ocean racing/cruising yacht, combining exceptional big-boat speed with luxurious accommodations. Built of fiberglass, the deck, cockpit, and cabin top are molded in one piece. She has a fin keel and spade rudder, and a Perkins Diesel with 2:1 reduction drives her along at nine knots. The three-cabin interior is finished in mahogany, and there are two fully enclosed heads. The main cabin sleeps four, the forward two, and the owner's stateroom aft, three. There is a special navigator's table and seat in the after cabin. All three cabins are accessible from the deck. The galley includes a hundred-pound ice chest, with room for a refrigeration unit.

Jensen Marine Corporation
235 Fischer Street
Costa Mesa, California 92626

CAPITAN 26

Length overall 26'3"
Length at waterline 19'
Beam 8'2"
Draft 4'
Sail area 301 square feet
Displacement 4300 pounds
CCA rating 22.4

This all-fiberglass sloop is a splendid family day sailer and overnighter. With a fin keel and masthead rig, she is fast, able, well balanced, and easy to handle. The cockpit is eight feet long and watertight. The cabin has V-berths forward, and twin quarter berths, toilet, and galley are optional to provide cruising accommodations for four. Capitan 26 has a watertight, ventilated well aft for outboard power. All in all, this is a well-designed boat, suitable for family sailing in exposed waters with comfort and safety.

Chris-Craft Corporation
P.O. Box 860
Pompano Beach, Florida 33061

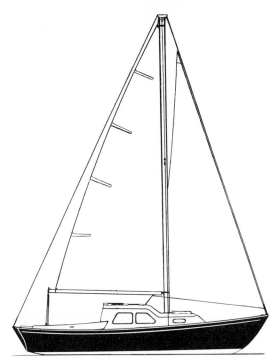

CAPRI 26

Length overall 26′3″
Length at waterline 19′
Beam 8′2″
Draft 4′
Sail area 301 square feet
Displacement 4800 pounds

The Capri 26 is a four-berth cruising auxiliary designed to meet MORC competition rules. It has the same hull and sailplan as the Capitan 26, but the cabin is larger and roomier. There are two quarter berths in the main cabin, and two forward. There is a convenient, complete galley to starboard, toilet and wardrobe to port, with 5′8″ headroom in main cabin. Interior trim is Philippine mahogany. She has outboard well aft, watertight and ventilated. A very able family boat for comfortable cruising or offshore racing.

Chris-Craft Corporation
P.O. Box 860
Pompano Beach, Florida 33061

CARAVELLE 42

Length overall 41'7"
Length at waterline 28'
Beam 11'
Draft 5'10"
Displacement 20,000 pounds
Sail area: yawl, 760 square feet;
    sloop, 755 square feet

The Caravelle 42 is high-quality auxiliary cruising-racing yacht, available either sloop- or yawl-rigged. Of good, wholesome design, she is a comfortable home afloat, and with a CCA rating of around 28.3, she is smart enough for offshore racing. While the hull is fiberglass, the interior is mahogany and teak finished in custom quality. She has accommodations for eight in two cabins, with two toilet rooms, and a most complete galley. The interior arrangement is actually custom-made to fit the owner's needs. Auxiliary power is a Gray 4-112.

John G. Alden and Company
89 Commercial Wharf
Boston, Massachusetts 02110

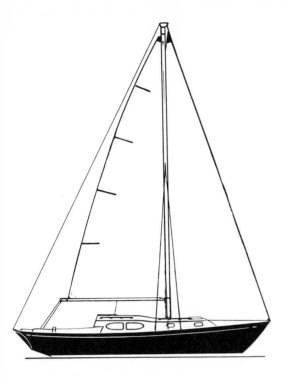

CHEROKEE 32

Length overall 32'
Length at waterline 22'6"
Beam 9'
Draft 5'1"
Sail area 434 square feet
Displacement 8698 pounds
CCA rating 25.2

This all-fiberglass cruising auxiliary was designed as a light-displacement, high-performance ocean racer. She has a fin keel and blade rudder, and for sail power she has a high aspect ratio and big foretriangle. Below there are sleeping accommodations for six, and the interior is finished in mahogany. The galley aft is convenient and efficient, with 6'3" headroom. The enclosed head has a hanging locker and vanity. Auxiliary power is a 30-hp Atomic Four. Spars and rigging are grounded to the keel. This sloop is a very smart sailer—close-winded and fast.

Chris-Craft Corporation
P.O. Box 860
Pompano Beach, Florida 33061

COASTER

Length overall 29'10"
Length at waterline 23'4"
Beam 9'4"
Draft 4'7"
Sail area 421 square feet
Displacement 9500 pounds
CCA rating 21.6

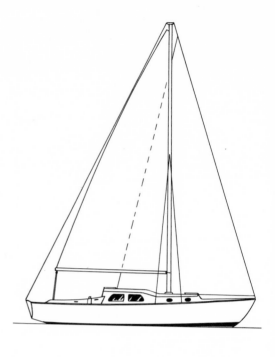

This ocean racing/cruising auxiliary has a long waterline and generous beam, with the ability to drive through heavy seas with an easy motion. With 3500 pounds of lead ballast in her keel and a long lateral plane, she is easy on the helm and very stable. The standard two-cabin interior sleeps five, with a complete galley aft. A dinette layout sleeps six, with the galley to starboard. Both arrangements have enclosed toilet room and plenty of lockers. Power is a Universal Atomic Four. The hull interior is covered with vinyl, and the trim is teak.

Pearson Yachts
West Shore Road
Portsmouth, Rhode Island 02871

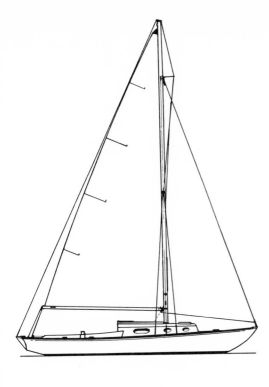

CONSTELLATION 30

Length overall 29'8"
Length at waterline 21'8"
Beam 8'
Draft 4'8"
Sail area 390 square feet
CCA rating 23.9
MORC rating 28

The Constellation is a fiberglass keel sloop for family cruising, day sailing, and racing. Large cockpit seats six or eight adults comfortably. Main cabin has four berths, full galley, enclosed head, and hanging locker. Auxiliary power is long-shaft cutboard, 9½ hp, in well. Spars are aluminum, with roller reefing boom. With 2750 pounds of lead ballast, she is stiff and able . . . and a smart sailer. For a family boat of moderate size and adequate accommodations, she is ideal.

Graves Yacht Yards
P.O. Box 36
Marblehead, Massachusetts 01945

CORINTHIAN 41 TRIMARAN

Length overall 41′
Beam 23′9″
Draft 26″
Sail area 625 square feet
Weight 9000 pounds

Perhaps the outstanding characteristic of a cruising trimaran is comfort. The Corinthian 41 can sleep eleven or twelve and sails on an even keel at all times. She is ketch-rigged for easy sail handling, rides through heavy offshore seas without pitching or rolling, yet can be sailed right up on a sandy beach. Accommodations are very roomy, with three separate cabins, two heads, an unbelievable amount of stowage space, and seven-foot headroom. The midships cockpit is roomy, sheltered, and dry. Power is a 55-hp Diesel, with a Martec folding prop.

Symons-Sailing, Inc.
Clocks Boulevard
Amityville, New York 11701

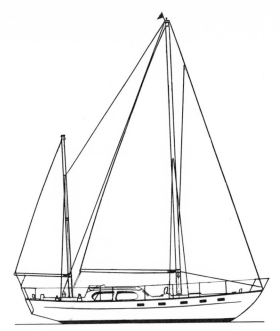

COUNTESS 44

Length overall 44'6"
Length at waterline 30'6"
Beam 12'
Draft 5'4"
Sail area 856 square feet
Displacement 28,000 pounds
CCA rating 29.1

The Countess 44 combines the virtues of a fast able ocean racer with the luxurious accommodations usually found in a motor sailer. The flush deck design gives plenty of footroom for sail handling, and the ketch rig makes her easy to balance when under short sail in heavy going. The large deckhouse gives outdoor protection and comfort in all weather. She sleeps six in three compartments, and four different arrangements are optional, to fit the owner's specific needs. Power is a 110-hp Diesel with 2:1 reduction.

Pearson Yachts
West Shore Road
Portsmouth, Rhode Island 02871

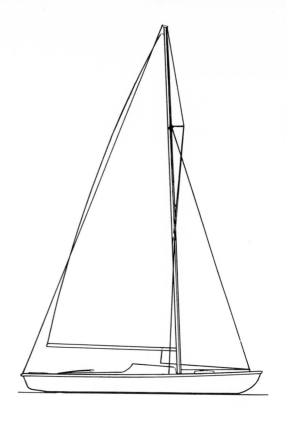

CRESCENT

Length overall 24'
Length at waterline 18'6"
Beam 7'
Draft 4'1"
Sail area 372 square feet
Displacement 2650 pounds
Keel ballast 1200 pounds

The Crescent is an all-fiberglass keel sloop designed primarily for racing, popular mainly in the Great Lakes area. There are two floor berths in the cabin and storage lockers. With a stove and head installed, it can accommodate two persons on weekend cruises or overnight trips. There is a hatch in the forward deck which is handy for sail handling, and an outboard well under a hatch in the afterdeck. All halyards and sheets can be reached without leaving the cockpit, which is a great convenience in heavy weather. Aluminum spars and roller reefing are standard equipment.

Customflex, Inc.
1817 Palmwood
Toledo, Ohio 43607

DOLPHIN

Length overall 24'2"
Length at waterline 19'
Beam 7'8"
Draft 5'10" centerboard down
Sail area 291 square feet

With a CCA rating of 19.4, the Dolphin is a successful racing/cruising sloop of fiberglass, with a centerboard housed in the keel. Cruising accommodations for four are comfortable. Galley includes stove, sink, icebox, and food locker. She has head, hanging locker, and cabin lights. Forward hatch gives ample ventilation. Inboard engine or outboard in well is optional, and the boat is trailable.

The O'Day Corporation
168 Stevens Street
Fall River, Massachusetts 02722

E←W

EAST WIND

Length overall 24'7"
Length at waterline 20'
Beam 7'1"
Draft 3'7"
Sail area 315 square feet
Displacement 4500 pounds
CCA rating 19.6

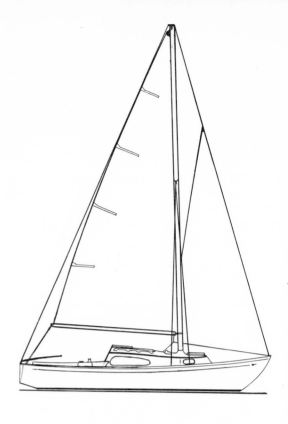

This fiberglass keel auxiliary was designed for family cruising and racing. With two thousand pounds of lead ballast in her keel, she is able, weatherly, and a smart sailer. The well-lighted main cabin has two transom berths, with galley aft. Forward cabin has two V-berths and a storage shelf. Toilet and hanging locker are separated from the forward and main cabins by two bulkheads and doors. Interior trim is mahogany. A one-cylinder, 8-hp Palmer supplies auxiliary power. Cockpit is self-bailing, with sail lockers under the seats.

Paceship, division of
Industrial Shipping Company, Ltd.
Mahone Bay, Nova Scotia, Canada

FORD 20

Length overall 20'
Beam 7'
Draft 8" to 5'
Sail area 205 square feet
Weight 950 pounds

The Ford 20 is designed for family day sailing or weekend cruising. The all-fiberglass hull has foamed-in-place flotation. The cockpit is spacious and comfortable for relaxed sailing, and the cuddy cabin provides stowage space and sleeping space for two, with room for optional head. Since the boat is easily trailered, the aluminum mast has a hinged mast step so it can be lowered quickly. The boom is fitted for roller reefing.

MFG Boat
P.O. Box 312
Union City, Pennsylvania 16438

GLADIATOR 24

Length overall 24'
Length at waterline 20'
Beam 7'6"
Draft 4'
Displacement 3850 pounds
Sail area 270 square feet
CCA rating 22.1
MORC rating 19.1
Pacific rating 246

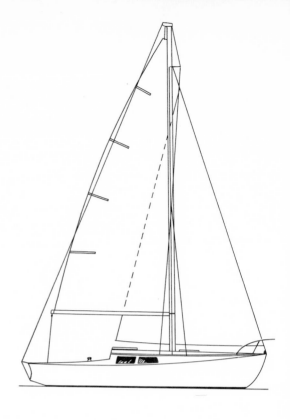

Designed as a compact blue-water cruiser-racer, the Gladiator 24 has a notable record for performance. She has won many trophies on the East and West coasts, and one was sailed from California to Hawaii in nineteen days. The fiberglass hull features raised deck construction, which gives added room below, and uncluttered deck space for sail handling. She has a large self-bailing cockpit for comfortable day sailing, and below deck are berths for four, a compact galley, head, and lockers. Spars are aluminum with roller-reefing boom.

Golden West Products
819 Harbor Drive
Redondo Beach, California 90277

GREENWICH 24

Length overall 24'3"
Length at waterline 17'5"
Beam 7'3"
Draft 3'
Sail area 225 square feet
Displacement 3825 pounds

With her classic lines, inboard sailplan, and shoal draft, this keel sloop is a wholesome day sailer-cruiser. With ample freeboard and beam, and a roomy cockpit, the Greenwich 24 is a comfortable family boat for relaxed sailing, and her shoal draft makes her ideal for gunkholing. Sleeps four in two cabins divided by bulkhead and hanging lockers. Toilet under berths in forward cabin, with curtain for privacy. Galley with sink and icebox is aft. All trim is teak. There is a well in afterdeck for an outboard. Aluminum spars with roller reefing.

Allied Boat Company, Inc.
Lower Main Street
Catskill, New York 12414

HINCKLEY 41

Length overall 41'2½"
Length at waterline 29'6"
Beam 10'2½"
Draft 6'1"
Sail area 677 feet
Displacement 18,000 pounds
Keel 6300 pounds
CCA rating 30.5

Long, lean, and powerful, this fiberglass auxiliary is ideal for the yachtsman who wants to race in fast company or cruise far and wide in comfort. The main cabin has two fixed berths and two transom berths. A roomy toilet room and hanging lockers close off the forward cabin, which has two berths, assuring privacy. A complete galley aft has three-burner stove and 200-pound icebox. Interior is mahogany and teak of custom quality. Gasoline engine or Diesel power is optional.

Henry R. Hinckley and Company
Southwest Harbor, Maine 04679

HINCKLEY 48

Length overall 48'5"
Length at waterline 34'6"
Beam 13'
Draft 5'3" centerboard up
Sail area: sloop, 1000 square feet;
    yawl, 1040 square feet
Displacement 35,500 pounds
CCA rating 36.9

The Hinckley 48 is the largest fiberglass production auxiliary built in this country, fitted for transoceanic racing or extended cruising. She has accommodations for eight, with forward and main cabins, and owner's stateroom aft. There are two toilet rooms with hot and cold showers. The large galley midships features a 9-cubic-foot refrigerator, with navigator's station and chart table adjoining. The keel houses a bronze centerboard which is operated electrically from the cockpit. A 35-hp Diesel engine pushes her along at seven knots.

Henry R. Hinckley and Company
Southwest Harbor, Maine 04679

HINCKLEY PILOT 35
(PILOT 35)

Length overall 35'9"
Length at waterline 25'
Beam 9'6"
Draft 5'
Sail area 554 square feet
Displacement 13,500 pounds

This modern fiberglass racing/cruising auxiliary is one of the finest of her size. With her clean lines, tall masthead rig, and a CCA rating of 26.5, she has an excellent racing record. Her interior is divided into two separate cabins, finished in mahogany and teak. Alternate layouts provide berths for four or six, and each cabin has its own entrance to the head. This is an excellent arrangement for two couples, or a family with children aboard. Auxiliary power is 25-hp Gray or Diesel at extra cost.

Henry R. Hinckley and Company
Southwest Harbor, Maine 04679

IMPERIAL 23

Length overall 22'6"
Length at waterline 20'
Beam 7'6"
Draft 2'9"
Sail area 220 square feet
Displacement 2688 pounds
MORC rating 18.0

Imperial 23 is an able offshore cruiser with twin bilge keels for shoal waters. The fiberglass hull is built to Lloyds specs and is self-righting with sails set. Accommodations include four berths, toilet in separate compartment, an excellent galley, and plenty of stowage space. She has a novel well aft in which an outboard can be easily lowered or raised. With short overhangs and a masthead rig, she is a smart sailer and very weatherly.

Wells Yachts, Inc.
50 Gregory Street
Marblehead, Massachusetts 01945

INVICTA II

Length overall 37'8"
Length at waterline 25'
Beam 10'8"
Draft 4'6" centerboard up
Displacement 17,750 pounds
Sail area: sloop, 605 square feet;
    yawl, 644 square feet
CCA rating: sloop, 25.1;
    yawl, 24.5

Available either sloop- or yawl-rigged, the Invicta II is a deep-water racing-cruising keel-centerboarder. With a low-profile cabin trunk, she has clean lines for looks and performance. She sleeps seven in two staterooms, with either the standard or dinette layout. Enclosed toilet and dressing room is very commodious. Galley has three-burner stove with oven. Power is Universal Atomic Four.

Pearson Yachts
West Shore Road
Portsmouth, Rhode Island 02871

KITTIWAKE

Length overall 23′7″
Length at waterline 17′9″
Beam 7′6″
Draft 2′11″
Sail area 248 square feet
Displacement 3700 pounds

This fiberglass keel sloop has a good-sized cockpit for day sailing, and cruising accommodations for four. With a masthead rig, fine lines, and a 1500-pound ballast keel, she is a smart sailer and weatherly. Spars are aluminum, with roller reefing. Below deck there are two quarter berths, galley, and icebox, and two V-berths forward with a toilet under a seat which can be curtained off for privacy. Headroom is 4′10″. Outboard well is the afterdeck. This would be a fine family boat for two adults and one or two small fry. Kits are available for home builders.

Kenner Boat Company, Inc.
P.O. Box 16
Knoxville, Arkansas 72845

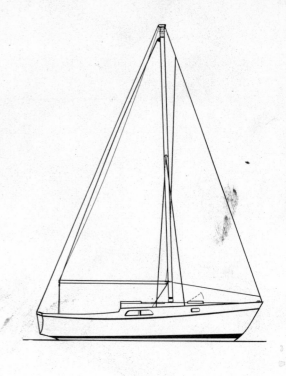

LARK

Length overall 24'
Length at waterline 18'6"
Beam 8'
Draft 4'
Sail area 283 square feet
Weight 4300 pounds
MORC rating 20.0

The Lark is an able, compact family cruiser with comfortable accommodations for four. With 1800 pounds of lead ballast in her keel, she is stiff and weatherly. The raised deck design gives maximum room below and provides a lounging area for the kids. There are two quarter berths, a galley to port, toilet and hanging locker to starboard, and a double berth forward with hatch over. The cockpit is roomy with plenty of legroom for relaxed day sailing. There is an outboard well in the afterdeck for auxiliary power.

Pearson Yachts
West Shore Road
Portsmouth, Rhode Island 02871

L/33

LUDERS 33

Length overall 33′
Length at waterline 24′
Beam 10′
Draft 5′
Sail area 529 square feet
Displacement 12,800 pounds
CCA rating 26.0

This racing/cruising auxiliary sloop is one of the fastest of her size. The fiberglass hull was tank tested before construction and she has proved to be a top racing contender. Living accommodations are roomy and comfortable, and she sleeps six in two separate cabins. The dinette in the main cabin converts to double berth. Enclosed toilet room has a shower, with large hanging locker opposite. Forward cabin has two berths, with full headroom in dressing area. Complete galley aft. Interior and exterior trim is teak. Power is 25-hp Gray.

Allied Boat Company
Lower Main Street
Catskill, New York 12414

MARINER

Length overall 19'2"
Length at waterline 17'9"
Beam 7'
Draft: centerboard model, 4'11";
  keel model, 3'3"
Sail area 185 square feet

Mariner is a compact day sailer-cruiser, with the same hull form as the Rhodes 19. Overnight cruising accommodations for two, and with a tent over the boom she can sleep two on the cockpit seats. Ideal for two adults and one or two small fry. Available in either keel or centerboard model. Has compact galley to port, and toilet under counter to starboard. Easy to trail and launch.

The O'Day Corporation
168 Stevens Street
Fall River, Massachusetts 02722

M 22

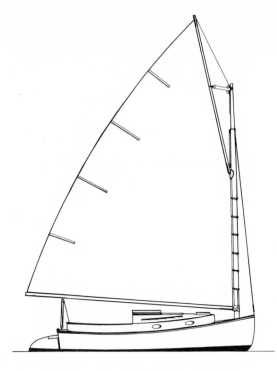

MARSHALL CAT

Length overall 22'2"
Length at waterline 21'4"
Beam 10'2"
Draft 2', centerboard up
Sail area 410 square feet
Displacement 5660 pounds

This is the classic Cape Cod catboat, famous in American tradition for three generations, reproduced line-for-line in fiberglass. With her traditional gaff rig and wide beam, no better family boat has been built. Her deep, wide cockpit keeps small fry safely inside and provides comfortable relaxed sailing for grown-ups. The roomy cabin has berths for four, a toilet and compact galley. Under the self-bailing cockpit floor is a 30-hp motor.

The Marshall Company
P.O. Box 266
South Dartmouth, Massachusetts 02748

MEDALIST 33

Length overall 33'
Length at waterline 24'
Beam 10'
Draft 5'3"
Sail area 467 square feet
Displacement 10,000 pounds
CCA rating 22

With her modern tall rig, short ballast keel, and spade rudder, the Medalist is a fast, close-winded, and weatherly racing/cruising auxiliary. She sleeps five in two cabins, with compact galley, enclosed head, and ample lockers. Variations in layout can be had, to suit the owner's needs. Has 30-hp Atomic Four for power, and keel has 4200 pounds of lead ballast. The interior is finished in hand-rubbed African mahogany, and all exterior joiner work is teak.

A. LeComte Company, Inc.
P.O. Box 117
New Rochelle, New York 10802

MERCER 44

Length overall 44'
Length at waterline 30'
Beam 11'9"
Draft: 4'3"; centerboard down, 9'
Sail area: yawl 902 square feet; sloop, 885
   square feet
Displacement 27,000 pounds

This fiberglass ocean racing/cruising yacht may be either sloop- or yawl-rigged. Her flush deck with doghouse makes for convenience in sail handling. With her tall rig and bronze centerboard in the keel, she is closed-winded and has plenty of drive. She has a seven-berth layout. Doghouse has quarter berth to port, and a roomy galley to port. Main cabin has four berths, drop-leaf table, dresser, desk, and chart table. Has roomy head with shower, double hanging lockers opposite. Forward cabin has two berths and seat. Gas or Diesel power is optional.

Cape Cod Shipbuilding Company
Narrows Road
Wareham, Massachusetts 02571

C/27

MOUNT DESERT C/27

Length overall 27'8"
Length at waterline 22'6"
Beam 7'11"
Draft 2'5"
Sail area 316 square feet
Displacement 4600 pounds

The C/27 is basically an enlarged version of the successful Amphibi-Con, and correspondingly has more room. She is constructed in both fiberglass and glued-strip models, and can be trailered. Main cabin has two berths, a complete galley, and portable table. Enclosed toilet, linen, and hanging lockers. Forward cabin has a large double berth. The 1400-pound ballast keel houses a centerboard. Eight-foot cockpit is self-bailing. Power optional outboard or inboard. Kits in various stages available for home building.

Mount Desert Yacht Yard, Inc.
Mount Desert, Maine 04660

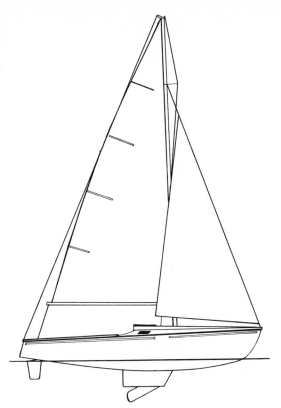

MUSTANG

Length overall 22′
Length at waterline 17′10″
Beam 7′
Draft: centerboard up, 28″;
   centerboard down, 5′3″
Displacement 1950 pounds
Sail area 247 square feet
MORC rating 19

The Mustang was designed for day sailing or weekend cruising and exploring. Of fiberglass with aluminum spars, she has a centerboard housed within a shallow fin keel. Cockpit is self-bailing. With two quarter berths and sleeping area forward, a toilet, stove, and sink, two adults and one or two small fry can be accommodated. An outboard motor on a transom bracket can be used for auxiliary power. The boat can be trailered easily, for greater utility.

Plastrend Corporation
9801 Jacksboro Highway
Fort Worth, Texas 76135

NORTHEAST 38

Length overall 38'3"
Length at waterline 26'8"
Beam 10'11"
Draft 5'4"
Sail area 596 square feet
Displacement 16,000 pounds
CCA rating 26.8

Rigged as a yawl or sloop, this yacht was designed for deep-water cruising and racing. She is built of fiberglass in Holland, and her construction, finish, equipment, and fittings are of custom yacht quality. She has the modern tall rig, short ballast keel, and spade rudder. Three different cabin layouts are available, with accommodations for six or seven in separate cabins. With hot water system, shower, fireplace, and ample tank capacity, a long ocean passage or extended cruise could be made in comfort. Gas engine or Diesel power is optional.

A. LeComte Company, Inc.
P.O. Box 117
New Rochelle, New York 10802

O/36

OHLSON 36

Length overall 36'3"
Length at waterline 25'6"
Beam 9'8"
Draft 5'
Sail area: yawl, 576 square feet;
    sloop, 555 square feet
Displacement 12,850 pounds
CCA rating: sloop, 25.6; yawl, 25.8

One of the fastest cruising auxiliaries of her size, the Ohlson 36 has a noteworthy record in ocean racing. She has a deep forefoot, sharp bow sections, unusually hard bilges, and a long, flat run. She has cruising accommodations for six—four berths in the main cabin and two forward. Roomy toilet room has a shower, and the galley aft is convenient and efficient. The interior of mahogany and teak is of custom quality. Power is a 25-hp Gray. Sloop or yawl rig is optional. The Ohlson 36 is not in production as this is written.

Campbell-Sheehan, Inc.
22 Boston Post Road
Larchmont, New York 10538

%41

OHLSON 41

Length overall 40'9"
Length at waterline 28'7"
Beam 11'
Draft 6'1"
Sail area: sloop, 750 square feet
Displacement 20,000 pounds

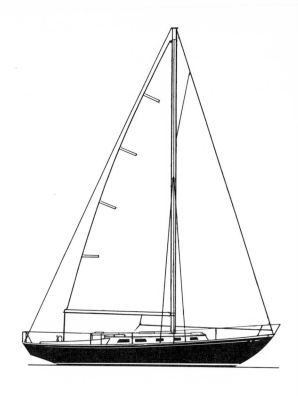

This fine racing/cruising auxiliary yacht is a gold-plater in every respect, with a choice of wood, steel, or aluminum. Able, fast, and stiff in a strong breeze, she would be ideal for ocean racing and extended deep-water cruising in comfort. Custom interior layout has seven berths, two in private owner's stateroom with head, four in main cabin, and one forward. Forward toilet room with shower extends the full width of the yacht. She has a very spacious U-shaped galley, and sizable navigator's table. Auxiliary power options to suit owner.

Campbell-Sheehan, Inc.
22 Boston Post Road
Larchmont, New York 10538

OUTLAW

Length overall 26′
Length at waterline 19′
Beam 8′
Draft 4′3″
Sail area 291 square feet
Displacement 5050 pounds
CCA rating 23
MORC rating 19.8

The Outlaw is a fiberglass keel sloop with masthead rig, designed as an all-around family boat for racing, cruising, and day sailing. She has a large, deep, self-bailing cockpit for sailing with comfort, and below deck are berths for four, galley, head, and stowage space. With a ballast keel of 2300 pounds and good freeboard, she is able, fast, and a dry sailer. She is equipped with an outboard well, but may be ordered with inboard engine installed.

The O'Day Corporation
168 Stevens Street
Fall River, Massachusetts 02722

PRIVATEER

Length overall 31'3"
Length at waterline 20'7"
Beam 8'
Draft 3'6"
Sail area 410 square feet
Displacement 6140 pounds

With her classic clipper bow and counter stern, Privateer is a traditional type produced in fiberglass. The boat is available with either the sloop or ketch rig, and in kit form for finishing yourself. A look at her underbody reveals a long lateral plane, which means she's steady on the helm and relaxing to sail. Below, there are four berths in two cabins, separated by galley and toilet room, with full headroom. Power is by outboard in a well. An excellent cruising boat for her size.

Kenner Boat Company, Inc.
P.O. Box 16
Knoxville, Arkansas 72845

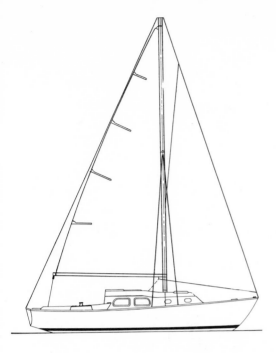

RENEGADE

Length overall 27'2"
Length at waterline 21'
Beam 8'7"
Draft 4'3"
Sail area 349 square feet
Displacement 6500 pounds
CCA rating 21.6
MORC rating 20.5

The Renegade is a fin-keel ocean racer with cruising accommodations for four. With a spade rudder and low wetted surface, she is sensitive on the helm, close-winded, and fast. The main cabin has two berths, with a full galley aft. The forward cabin has two V-berths, and can be closed off from the main cabin for privacy. She has an enclosed head and hanging lockers. Outboard motor is well aft; inboard motor is optional. Interior trim is mahogany.

Pearson Yachts
West Shore Road
Portsmouth, Rhode Island 02871

161

SCHOCK 25

Length overall 25′
Length at waterline 16′4″
Beam 7′
Maximum draft 4′1″
Sail area 222 square feet
Displacement 2200 pounds

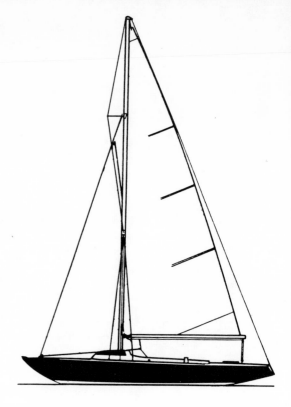

The S-25 is an all-fiberglass one-design keel sloop for racing or family day sailing. Since she has a large cockpit and ample deck area, eight can sail in comfort. Cuddy cabin has two berths and a toilet, for overnight trips. With 1100 pounds of ballast in the fin keel, she is a very able, high-performance boat suitable for open waters. She has flotation tanks and an outboard well, and can be trailered.

W. D. Schock Company
3502 South Greenville Street
Santa Ana, California 92704

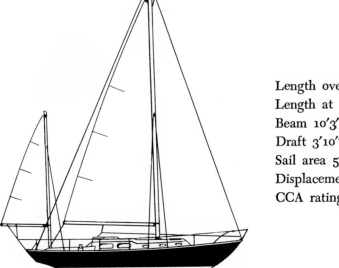

SEABREEZE 35

Length overall 34'6"
Length at waterline 24'
Beam 10'3"
Draft 3'10"
Sail area 575 square feet
Displacement 13,600 pounds
CCA rating 26.5

This keel-centerboard cruising yacht is available with either yawl or sloop rig. Stiff and dry in a fresh breeze, she is seakindly, and suitable for long ocean passages and offshore racing. There are two optional cabin arrangements for sleeping six—the standard layout with extension berths, and the convertible dinette layout. The enclosed head has a shower, and the galley aft is most complete. Interior trim is teak. Centerboard housed in the keel is handled by a winch in the cockpit. Power is 25-hp Gray, or Diesel optional.

Allied Boat Company, Inc.
Lower Main Street
Catskill, New York 12414

SEAFARER-23
(formerly KESTREL)

Length overall 23′1″
Length at waterline 16′9″
Beam 7′2″
Displacement 3700 pounds
Sail area 235 square feet
CCA rating 16.5

Versatility is the main characteristic of this fiberglass keel cruiser. There are five optional layouts to choose from. One features a long cockpit with two berths and a head below, for day sailing or overnight trips. The others have conventional arrangements with berths and cruising accommodations for four. The long ballast keel houses a centerboard, and there is a well in the afterdeck to take an outboard. She can easily be trailered, and stored in your backyard.

Seafarer Fiberglass Yachts, Inc.
414 New York Avenue
Huntington, New York 11743

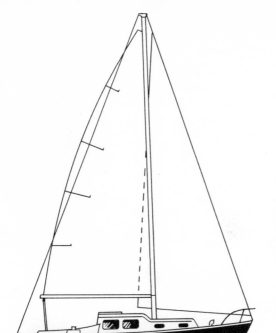

SEAFARER-26
(formerly MERIDIAN)

Length overall 25'7"
Length at waterline 17'9"
Beam 7'3"
Displacement 5500 pounds
Draft 3'7"
Sail area 300 square feet
CCA rating 17
MORC rating 18

Seafarer-26 (formerly Meridian) is a fiber-glass auxiliary keel sloop for family cruising and racing. With a long keel for directional stability, a high ballast ratio for stiffness, and a masthead rig, she is an able, comfortable boat for relaxed sailing. Six variations of the basic design provide accommodations for four, with full headroom in the cabin. One model is designed as a day sailer, with a long cockpit seating eight. There is a well in the afterdeck for outboard power.

Seafarer Fiberglass Yachts, Inc.
414 New York Avenue
Huntington, New York 11743

SEAFARER-31

Length overall 31'
Length at waterline 21'
Beam 8'9"
Draft 4'7"
Displacement 8800 pounds
Sail area 413 square feet
CCA rating 20

This excellent ocean racer is made in six different models with luxurious living accommodations for up to six, either sloop- or yawl-rigged. All models have full headroom, enclosed head, a complete galley, and an abundance of lockers, bins, and drawers for stowage. Interior arrangements are custom-built to suit the needs of the individual owner. Though a well is provided for outboard power, an inboard engine can be installed as an optional extra.

Seafarer Fiberglass Yachts, Inc.
414 New York Avenue
Huntington, New York 11743

SEAWIND 30

Length overall 30'6"
Length at waterline 24'
Beam 9'3"
Draft 4'4"
Sail area: sloop, 400 square feet; ketch, 500
    square feet
Displacement 12,080 pounds

This fiberglass cruising ketch is notable for ease of handling and cruising comfort. With her long keel and outboard rudder, she is steady on the helm and relaxing to sail. The cockpit is large and deep, and the decks are wide. There are four berths, with a double stateroom forward and two berths in the main cabin. Enclosed head has basin, counter, and linen hamper, with hanging locker opposite. Galley aft has ample counter area. Two couples can cruise with comfort and privacy. Power is Gray Sea Scout, and a sloop rig is optional.

Allied Boat Company, Inc.
Lower Main Street
Catskill, New York 12414

SIGNET 20

Length overall 19'10"
Length at waterline 16'
Beam 6'8"
Draft: fin keel, 3'; twin keel, 2'
Sail area 192 square feet
Displacement 2146 pounds
MORC rating: fin keel, 16.3; twin keels, 15.2

The Signet is an American-designed, British-built fiberglass cruising sloop, available with a fin keel or twin bilge keels. An outboard well is fitted, for auxiliary power, and the cockpit is self-bailing. With galley and toilet, she has overnight accommodations for four adults, or extended cruising for two. Spars are aluminum, and she carries a masthead genoa jib and spinnaker. Eight hundred pounds of outside ballast is carried, and she conforms to MORC requirements.

Signet Marine Division
S. L. Kaye Company
230 Fifth Avenue
New York, New York 10001

CS 25

SOUTH COAST 25

Length overall 25'6"
Length at waterline 20'6"
Beam 8'
Draft 3'6"
Sail area 310 square feet
Displacement 4200 pounds

This cruising sailboat, with accommodations for five, is one of the roomiest for her size on the market. With a fin keel and spade rudder, she is able and weatherly, and the raised-deck design makes for dry sailing. Below, a dinette converts to a double berth, with a quarter berth and convenient galley opposite. The fully enclosed head gives maximum privacy. There are a clothes hamper and a hanging locker opposite. Folding doors give access to the forward cabin, which has two berths. The large main hatch can be raised to give maximum ventilation and 6'1" headroom. The standard model has an outboard well, but an inboard motor can be fitted at extra cost.

South Coast Seacraft
P.O. Box 1674
Shreveport, Louisiana 71102

SOVEREL MORC RACER

Length overall 28'7"
Length at waterline 23'2"
Draft 2'10"
Sail area 360 square feet
Displacement 6000 pounds

The MORC Racer has been adapted from the Soverel 28 hull for those who are more interested in racing and day sailing. Up to eight people can be seated in the nine-foot cockpit. In the cabin are limited living space for four, and galley and enclosed head, which makes her ideal for weekend cruising. Inboard or outboard power is optional. The boat can easily be car-trailered. The Soverel MORC Racer is no longer being advertised for sale.

Soverel Marine, Inc.
2225 Idle Wilde Road
North Palm Beach, Florida 33403

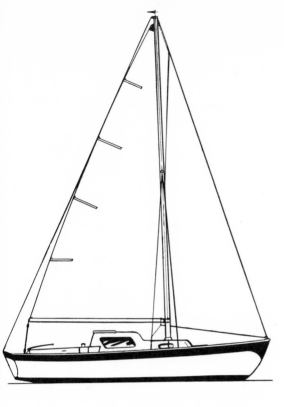

SOVEREL 28

Length overall 28'8"
Length at waterline 24'
Beam 8'4"
Draft 2'11"
Sail area: 480 square feet, sloop or yawl
Displacement 7000 pounds
CCA rating 26
MORC rating 24

Available with either sloop or yawl rig, the Soverel 28 is one of the best sailing auxiliaries under thirty feet. The fiberglass hull has a shallow keel housing a centerboard, and 1500 pounds of lead ballast. The cabin has full headroom, four berths, enclosed head, complete galley, and hanging locker. Power is 30-hp inboard, or optional outboard. With her light displacement, long waterline, and straight run, she is a fast sailer, and has an excellent racing record. Her shoal draft permits exploring many waters forbidden to others, yet she is capable of extended offshore cruising with comfort and safety.

Soverel Marine, Inc.
2225 Idle Wilde Road
North Palm Beach, Florida 33403

173

SOVEREL 36

Length overall 36'7"
Length at waterline 29'
Beam 11'
Draft 4'6"
Displacement 18,000 pounds
Sail area: 837 square feet, sloop or yawl
CCA rating 32

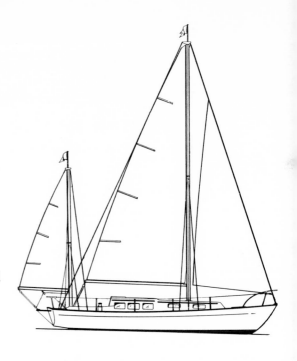

This shoal-draft fiberglass yacht combines shoal draft, generous beam, and long waterline for comfortable, relaxed, family cruising, or blue-water racing and extended cruising. Though designed for cruising comfort for four, the yacht has a total of seven berths. Forward cabin can be closed for privacy. Head has full standing room, linen locker, and shower. There is a dinette and settee for relaxing, and ample galley and chart table aft. Auxiliary power is 30 hp. Optional masthead sloop or yawl rig.

Soverel Marine, Inc.
2225 Idle Wilde Road
North Palm Beach, Florida 33403

$\overset{\text{S}}{31}$

SUMNERCRAFT 31

Length overall 31'
Length at waterline 27'
Beam 10'2"
Draft 3'1"
Sail area 380 square feet

Designed for extended cruising in comfort, this motor sailer is of fiberglass-and-wood sandwich construction. Powered with a 108-hp Diesel motor, she has a cruising range of two thousand to three thousand miles at 6.3 knots. Because of her moderate sail area and double headsails, she can easily be handled by one man. Accommodations are unusually roomy, sleeping six or eight in two cabins. The hull has plastic foam flotation, and is self-righting.

Sumner Boat Company, Inc.
334 South Bayview Avenue
Amityville, New York 11701

TARTAN 27

Length overall 27′
Length at waterline 21′5″
Beam 8′7½″
Draft 3′2″
Displacement 6875 pounds
Sail area: sloop, 372 square feet; yawl, 394
   square feet
CCA rating 20.2

From the standpoint of sailing ability and cruising comfort, this fiberglass auxiliary is one of the best of her size. She sleeps five in two cabins separated by the enclosed head. In the main cabin, a dinette converts to a double berth, with a quarter berth opposite. The galley is convenient, and the icebox fills from the deck. Power is 30-hp Atomic Four. A fiberglass centerboard is housed in the ballast keel. The masthead rig gives generous-sized headsails when racing as a sloop. She is easy to handle when cruising short-handed as a yawl.

Douglass and McLeod, Inc.
P.O. Box 311
Painesville, Ohio 44077

TEMPEST

Length overall 23'2"
Length at waterline 17'
Beam 7'8"
Draft 3'9"
Sail area 211 square feet
Displacement 3000 pounds
CCA rating 21

With a 1250-pound fin keel and a masthead rig, the Tempest is a smart, fast sailer for one-design racing or short cruises. Average MORC rating is 18.5. She has a self-bailing, eight-foot cockpit, and forward hatch for ventilation. Separate head enclosure and galley area with molded-in icebox. This boat is very responsive to the helm and has good stability for heavy weather. An outboard motor can be used on transom bracket for auxiliary power.

The O'Day Corporation
168 Stevens Street
Fall River, Massachusetts 02722

TRITON

Length overall 28'6"
Length at waterline 20'6"
Beam 8'3"
Draft 4'
Sail area: sloop, 362 square feet; yawl, 400 square feet
Displacement 8400 pounds
CCA rating: sloop, 20.6; yawl, 20.9

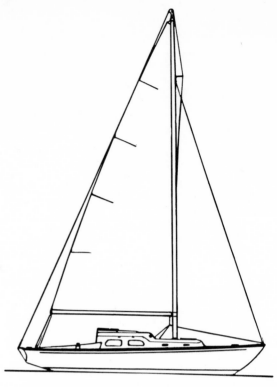

The Triton has the distinction of being the first full-size, one-design racing/cruising auxiliary produced on a large scale, and today she is the largest cruising class, numbering over seven hundred, with active fleets on both the East and West coasts. Though a yawl rig is optional, the majority are sloops, with the seven-eighths headsail rig. The main cabin has two berths, with the galley aft. Enclosed toilet room gives privacy, and access to the forward cabin, which has two berths and a seat, with hatch over. Auxiliary power is a Universal Atomic Four.

Pearson Yachts
West Shore Road
Portsmouth, Rhode Island 02871

TYLERCRAFT 24

Length overall 24'
Length at waterline 20'
Beam 7'5"
Draft 2'
Sail area 243 square feet
Displacement 4000 pounds

This is a very compact day sailer, ocean cruiser-racer, with accommodations for two or four. She has twin ballasted fixed keels, is noncapsizable and self-righting. She will sit bolt-upright on the keels when beached or hauled out, without cradle or shoring. The self-bailing cockpit is nine feet long. Three different interior layouts can be had, incorporating features usually found on much larger boats, such as an enclosed head with sliding doors. Power is an outboard, with jet-drive optional. With a rating of 18.6, the T-24 has an excellent MORC racing record. Four-wheel tandem trailer is available.

Tylercraft, Inc.
1439 Montauk Highway
Oakdale, New York 11769

VANGUARD

Length overall 32′6½″
Length at waterline 22′4″
Beam 9′3″
Draft 4′6″
Sail area: sloop, 470 square feet; yawl, 496
  square feet
Displacement 10,300 pounds
CCA rating: sloop, 22.1; yawl, 22.2

Either yawl- or sloop-rigged, the Vanguard has an excellent record in offshore racing and extended cruising. With a high displacement ratio and ample ballast, she is very stable in heavy going and a smart sailer. She sleeps six in two separate staterooms, has an enclosed head with access fore and aft, and numerous lockers and stowage facilities. Cabins are light and well ventilated. Dinette arrangement in main cabin is optional. Floor and interior trim is teak. Auxiliary power is a Universal Atomic Four.

Pearson Yachts
West Shore Road
Portsmouth, Rhode Island 02871

VIVACITY

Length overall 20'
Length at waterline 17'6"
Beam 7'
Draft 2'4"
Sail area 175 square feet
Displacement 1800 pounds
MORC rating 15

Vivacity is a fiberglass family cruising or MORC racing sloop. She has twin ballast keels which give shoal draft and stiffness in sailing and make her self-righting in case of a knockdown. There are berths for four, a toilet, and galley. The cockpit is self-bailing. Spars are aluminum with roller reefing. The transom has a bracket for an outboard motor. This is a very seaworthy craft, close-winded and weatherly. She is easily trailered, and with the twin keels needs no cradle.

Wells Yachts Inc.
50 Gregory Street
Marblehead, Massachusetts 01945

WANDERER

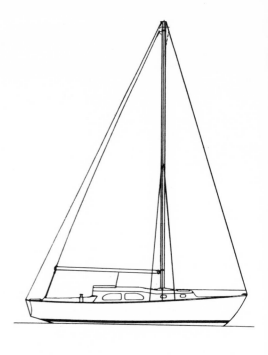

Length overall 30′3″
Length at waterline 23′4″
Beam 9′4″
Draft 3′6″ centerboard up
Sail area 421 square feet
Displacement 9800 pounds
CCA rating 21.8

The Wanderer is a versatile centerboarder. With her long keel and shoal draft, she can cruise where the water is thin. With her board down, the masthead rig on a long lean hull gives her the drive and speed for offshore racing. Her accommodations are roomy and convenient, with optional layouts. The standard layout sleeps five, in two cabins. The dinette arrangement, with two quarter berths, sleeps six. The galley layout is very convenient. Enclosed head and hanging locker separate the two cabins. Auxiliary power is a Universal Atomic Four.

Pearson Yachts
West Shore Road
Portsmouth, Rhode Island 02871

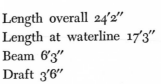

WEEKENDER

Length overall 24'2"
Length at waterline 17'3"
Beam 6'3"
Draft 3'6"
Sail area 218 square feet
Displacement 2150 pounds

The Weekender is the cruising version of the Rainbow. It has the same hull, rig, and sailplan. With a larger cabin and shorter cockpit, there is room for four berths, a head, sink, and icebox. The doghouse provides sitting headroom, and a forward hatch gives ventilation. Thus the Weekender can be a family cruiser, and in addition, an ocean racer, since she meets all MORC requirements. Auxiliary power could be had with an outboard, since there is a lazarette with a large hatch in the afterdeck. The Weekender is no longer in production.

Tidewater Boats, Inc.
P.O. Box 1571
Annapolis, Maryland 21404

WESTWIND

Length overall 23'11"
Length at waterline 18'2"
Beam 7'11¼"
Draft: centerboard up, 2'1¼"; centerboard
  down, 5'6"
Sail area 304 square feet
Displacement 4670 pounds
CCA rating 18.4
MORC rating 21

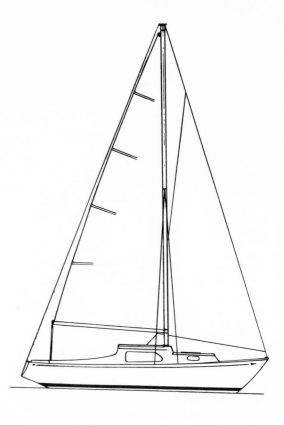

This compact centerboarder was designed for family cruising and day sailing. With her shoal draft she is ideal for gunkholing and exploring strange waters, and she can be trailered. There are four berths in the cabin, with a toilet installed between the forward berths. The galley is compact, with stainless steel sink and fiberglass icebox. Auxiliary power is a 6-hp outboard carried in self-bailing well. Spars are aluminum, with roller reefing.

Paceship, division of
Industrial Shipping Company, Ltd.
Mahone Bay, Nova Scotia, Canada

AURORA 21
21′×16′×6′4″×3′3″. Sail area 185 square feet. Sloop. Displacement 1800 pounds. Fiberglass hull, aluminum spars. Two berths. Head optional. Auxiliary power optional.

Wesco Marine
8211 Lankershim Boulevard
North Hollywood, California 91605

BERMUDA 40
40′9″×27′10″×11′9″×4′1″ (centerboard up). Sail area 725 square feet. Yawl rig. Displacement 19,000 pounds. CCA rating 28.4. Fiberglass hull, aluminum spars. Two cabins, six berths. Galley and head. Auxiliary power 35 hp.

Henry R. Hinckley and Company
Southwest Harbor, Maine 04679

BLUE JACKET
22′10″×17′6″×7′1″×3′9″. Sail area 201 square feet. Sloop. Displacement 2900 pounds. Fiberglass hull, aluminum spars. Two berths. Head optional. Auxiliary power optional.

Paceship, division of
Industrial Shipping Company, Ltd.
Mahone Bay, Nova Scotia, Canada

CAL-2-24
24′×19′2″×7′9″×4′. Sail area 274 square feet. Sloop. Displacement 3700 pounds. Fiberglass hull, aluminum spars. Two cabins, four berths. Head including galley optional. Auxiliary power optional.

Jensen Marine
235 Fischer Street
Costa Mesa, California 92626

CAL 28
28′×22′6″×9′×4′6″. Sail area 355 square feet. Sloop. Displacement 6000 pounds. CCA rating 25.6. Fiberglass hull, aluminum spars. Two cabins, six berths, galley, and head. Auxiliary power optional.

Jensen Marine
235 Fischer Street
Costa Mesa, California 92626

CHALLENGER
24′4″×18′×3′4″. Sail area 289 square feet. Sloop. Displacement 3930 pounds. CCA rating 18.2. Fiberglass hull, aluminum spars. Two cabins, four berths, and galley. Head optional. Auxiliary power optional.

Columbia Yacht Corporation
275 McCormick Avenue
Costa Mesa, California 92626

COLUMBIA 26
26″×19′×8″×3′5″. Sail area 321 square feet. Displacement 5200 pounds. CCA rating 20.5. Fiberglass hull, aluminum spars. Two cabins, four berths, galley, and head. Auxiliary power optional.

Columbia Yacht Corporation
275 McCormick Avenue
Costa Mesa, California 92626

COLUMBIA 28

27′7″×21′8′×8′6″×4′4″. Sail area 343
square feet. Sloop. Displacement 5800
pounds. CCA rating 24. Fiberglass hull,
aluminum spars. Two cabins, six berths.
Dinette, galley, and head. Auxiliary
power optional.

Columbia Yacht Corporation
275 McCormick Avenue
Costa Mesa, California 92626

CONTROVERSY 36

37′1″×31′6″×10′1″×5′6″. Sail area
550 square feet. Yawl. Displacement
13,500 pounds. Wood hull, wood
spars. Three cabins, seven berths,
galley, and head. Auxiliary power
optional.

Mount Desert Yacht Yards
Mount Desert, Maine 04660

COLUMBIA 34

34′×23′7″×9′11″×8′. Sail area 476
square feet. Displacement 10,000
pounds. Fiberglass hull, aluminum
spars. Two cabins, six berths. Galley
and head. Auxiliary power 30-hp
Atomic Four.

Columbia Yacht Corporation
275 McCormick Avenue
Costa Mesa, California 92626

EXCALIBUR 26

25′11″×21′8″×7′9″×4′8″. Sail area 302
square feet. Sloop. Displacement 3770
pounds. Fiberglass hull, aluminum spars.
Two cabins, four berths. Galley and
head. Auxiliary power optional.

Islander Yachts
777 West Seventeenth Street
Costa Mesa, California 92627

COLUMBIA 40

39′2″×27′×10′8″×4′6″, centerboard up.
Sail area 673 square feet. Sloop.
Displacement 20,200 pounds. Fiberglass
hull, aluminum spars. Two cabins, six
berths, galley, and head. Auxiliary
power 30-hp Atomic four.

Columbia Yacht Corporation
275 McCormick Avenue
Costa Mesa, California 92626

FIREBIRD

19′5″×17′10″×6′7″×1′4″, centerboard
up. Sail area 199 square feet. Sloop.
Displacement 1060 pounds. Fiberglass
hull, aluminum spars. One cabin, four
berths. Galley and head optional.
Auxiliary power optional.

Nautica Corporation
P.O. Box 26
Paramus, New Jersey 07652

COMANCHE 42

42′×30′4″×10′10″×6′6″. Sail area 740
square feet. Sloop. Displacement 17,641
pounds. CCA rating 36.2. Fiberglass
hull, aluminum spars. One cabin, seven
berths, galley, and head. Auxiliary
power 30 hp.

Chris-Craft Corporation
P.O. Box 860
Pompano Beach, Florida 33061

FOLKDANCER

27′×19′8″×7′6″×4′. Sail area 296
square feet. Sloop. Displacement 5040
pounds. Fiberglass hull, aluminum
spars. Two cabins, six berths. Galley
and head. Auxiliary power 5 hp.

Wells Yachts Inc.
50 Gregory Street
Marblehead, Massachusetts 01945

HR 28

28'3"×20'9"×8'6"×4'. Sail area 354 square feet. Sloop. Displacement 6700 pounds. CCA rating 23.8. Fiberglass hull, aluminum spars. One cabin, four berths, galley, and head. Auxiliary power optional.

Hinterhoeller, Ltd.
526 Regent Street
Niagara-on-the-Lake, Ontario, Canada

IRWIN 24

24'×18'6"×8'×3'6". Sail area 275 square feet. Sloop. Displacement 3000 pounds. MORC rating 20.1. Fiberglass hull, aluminum spars. Two cabins, four berths, galley, and head. Auxiliary power optional.

Irwin Yachts
13055 Forty-ninth Street North
St. Petersburg, Florida 33732

IRWIN 27

27'1"×20'6"×8'8"×2'8", centerboard up. Sail area 356 square feet. Sloop. Displacement 6600 pounds. CCA rating 22. Fiberglass hull, aluminum spars. Two cabins, four or five berths, galley, and head. Auxiliary power optional.

Irwin Yachts
13055 Forty-ninth Street North
St. Petersburg, Florida 33732

IRWIN 31

31'1"×22'3"×9'7"×3'4", centerboard up. Sail area 460 square feet. Fiberglass hull, aluminum spars. Two cabins, six berths, galley, and head. Auxiliary power 30 hp.

Irwin Yachts
13055 Forty-ninth Street North
St. Petersburg, Florida 33732

ISLANDER 21

20'10"×18'×7'10"×3'4". Sail area 208 square feet. Sloop. Displacement 1950 pounds. Fiberglass hull, aluminum spars. Two cabins, four berths, galley, and head. Auxiliary power optional.

Islander Yachts
777 West Seventeenth Street
Costa Mesa, California 92627

ISLANDER BAHAMA 24

24'×20'×7'10"×3'5". Sail area 296 square feet. Sloop. Displacement 3400 pounds. CCA rating 18.2. Fiberglass hull, aluminum spars. Two cabins, four berths, galley, and head. Auxiliary power optional.

Islander Yachts
777 West Seventeenth Street
Costa Mesa, California 92627

ISLANDER 27

26'8"×20'×8'×4'. Sail area 325 square feet. Sloop. Displacement 4100 pounds. CCA rating 22.4. Fiberglass hull, aluminum spars. Two cabins, four berths, galley, and head. Auxiliary power optional.

Islander Yachts
777 West Seventeenth Street
Costa Mesa, California 92627

ISLANDER 30

29'7"×23'4"×8'10"×3'8". Sail area 359 square feet. Sloop. Displacement 7200 pounds. CCA rating 25.9. Fiberglass hull, aluminum spars. Two cabins, six berths, galley, and head. Auxiliary power 30 hp.

Islander Yachts
777 West Seventeenth Street
Costa Mesa, California 92627

ISLANDER 33

32'7"×24'×10'2"×4'6". Sail area 476 square feet. Sloop. Displacement 10,000 pounds. CCA rating 26.9. Fiberglass hull, aluminum spars. Two cabins, seven berths. Galley and head. Auxiliary power 30 hp.

Islander Yachts
777 West Seventeenth Street
Costa Mesa, California 92627

ISLANDER 44

43'10"×32'6"×11'×5'10". Sail area 774 square feet. Sloop. Displacement 22,500 pounds. CCA rating 38.1. Fiberglass hull, aluminum spars. Two cabins, eight berths, galley, and head. Auxiliary power optional.

Islander Yachts
777 West Seventeenth Street
Costa Mesa, California 92627

MORGAN 24

24'11½"×21'6"×8'×2'9", centerboard up. Sail area 310 square feet. Sloop. Displacement 4900 pounds. CCA rating 21.8. MORC rating 20.8. Fiberglass hull, aluminum spars. Two cabins, four berths, galley, and head. Auxiliary power optional.

Morgan Yacht Corporation
2501 Seventy-second Street North
St. Petersburg, Florida 33710

MORGAN 34

34'×24'9"×10'×3'3", centerboard up. Sail area 550 square feet. Sloop. Displacement 12,500 pounds. CCA rating 26.3. Fiberglass hull, aluminum spars. Two cabins, six berths, galley, and head. Auxiliary power 30 hp.

Morgan Yacht Corporation
2501 Seventy-second Street North
St. Petersburg, Florida 33710

MORGAN 41

41'×30'×11'3"×4'2", centerboard up. Sail area 775 square feet. Sloop. Displacement 19,500 pounds. Fiberglass hull, aluminum spars. Two or three cabins, six berths. Auxiliary power 30 hp.

Morgan Yacht Corporation
2501 Seventy-second Street North
St. Petersburg, Florida 33710

MORGAN 45

45'8"×31'5"×11'×6'1". Sail area 895 square feet. Sloop. Displacement 25,000 pounds. CCA rating 35.2. Fiberglass hull, aluminum spars. Two cabins, eight berths, galley, and head. Auxiliary power 40 hp.

Morgan Yacht Corporation
2501 Seventy-second Street North
St. Petersburg, Florida 33710

NANTUCKET 33

33'×26'×10'2"×5'4". Sail area 488 square feet. Sloop. Displacement 10,000 pounds. Aluminum hull and spars. Three cabins, five berths, galley, and head. Auxiliary power 12 hp.

Campbell-Sheehan, Inc.
22 Boston Post Road
Larchmont, New York 10538

OHLSON 44

43'6"×30'5"×11'6"×6'6". Sail area 843 square feet. Sloop. Displacement 24,500 pounds. Steel, wood, or aluminum hull. Spruce spars. Three cabins, seven berths, galley, and head. Auxiliary power optional.

Campbell-Sheehan, Inc.
22 Boston Post Road
Larchmont, New York 10538

PEARSON 35

35′×25′×10′×3′9″, centerboard up. Sail area 550 square feet. Sloop or yawl. Displacement 13,000 pounds. Fiberglass hull, aluminum spars. Two cabins, six berths, galley, and head. Auxiliary power 30 hp.

Pearson Yachts
West Shore Road
Portsmouth, Rhode Island 02871

PEARSON 43

42′9″×31′3″×11′9″×6′3″. Sail area 825 square feet. Sloop or yawl. Displacement 21,796 pounds. Fiberglass hull, aluminum spars. Three cabins, eight berths, galley, and head. Auxiliary power 30 hp.

Pearson Yachts
West Shore Road
Portsmouth, Rhode Island 02871

SABRE

32′5″×22′7″×6′3″×4′4″. Sail area 347 square feet. Sloop. Displacement 4500 pounds. CCA rating 27. Fiberglass hull, aluminum spars. Two cabins, four berths, galley, and head. Auxiliary power optional.

Columbia Yacht Corporation
275 McCormick Avenue
Costa Mesa, California 92626

SHARK

24′×20′×6′11″×3′. Sail area 190 square feet. Sloop. Displacement 2200 pounds. MORC rating 20. Fiberglass hull, aluminum spars. One cabin, four berths, galley, and head. Auxiliary power optional.

Hinterhoeller, Ltd.
526 Regent Street
Niagara-on-the-Lake,
Ontario, Canada

TARTAN 34

34′5″×25′×10′2″×3′11″, centerboard up. Sail area 515 square feet. Sloop or yawl. Displacement 11,200 pounds. CCA rating 27.5. Fiberglass hull, aluminum spars. Two cabins, five berths, galley, and head. Auxiliary power 30 hp.

Douglass and McLeod, Inc.
P.O. Box 311
Painesville, Ohio 44077

TARTAN 37

37′×25′6″×10′6″×3′10″, centerboard up. Sail area 618 square feet. Sloop or yawl. Displacement 15,700 pounds. CCA rating 28.5. Fiberglass hull, aluminum spars. Two cabins, six berths, galley, and head. Auxiliary power 30 hp.

Douglass and McLeod, Inc.
P.O. Box 311
Painesville, Ohio 44077

TAVANA 33

33′×26′×10′×3′, centerboard up. Sail area: sloop, 500 square feet; yawl, 550 square feet. Displacement 11,000 pounds. CCA rating 22.3 Fiberglass hull, wood spars. Accommodations and auxiliary power optional. Available in kit form for home builders.

Glander Boats, Inc.
11320 S.W. 208th Drive
Miami, Florida 33157

THUNDERBIRD

26′×19′×7′6″×4′9″. Sail area 264 square feet. Sloop. Displacement 3900 pounds. CCA rating 25. Plywood hull, wood spars. One cabin, four berths, galley, and head. Auxiliary power 10 hp. Available in kit form for home builders.

Superior Marine Company
Center Line, Michigan 48015

TRIANGLE 32

32′×26′8″×10′×3′5″. Sail area 480 square feet. Auxiliary cruising ketch. Displacement 12,000 pounds. One cabin, double berth, galley, dinette, head. Two centerboards.

Grampian Marine Ltd.
451 Woody Road
Oakville, Ontario, Canada

VENTURE

21′×18′6″×6′10″×1′6″, centerboard up. Sail area 265 square feet. Sloop. Displacement 1200 pounds. MORC rating 25.1. Fiberglass hull, aluminum spars. One cabin, four berths, galley, and head optional. Auxiliary power optional.

MacGregor Yachts, Inc.
817 West Seventeenth Street
Costa Mesa, California 92627

190

Photograph credits gratefully acknowledged:

W. H. Ballard, South West Harbor, Maine,
     pages 154 and 156
Beckner Photo Service, P.O. Box 411, Balboa Island,
     California, pages 74 and 162
Agnew Fisher, Buckfield Lane, Greenwich, Connecticut,
     page 141
Norman Fortier, 52 Elm Street, South Dartmouth,
     Massachusetts, page 180
Morrison–Gottlieb Inc., 40 East 49th Street, New York
     City 10017, pages 44, 45, and 139
Morris Rosenfeld & Sons, 116 Nassau Street, New York
     City 10038, pages 152 and 184
R. H. Townsend, 1215 Essex Lane, Newport Beach,
     California, page 80
Wamboldt–Waterfield Photography Limited, 2856
     Gottingen Street, Halifax, Nova Scotia, page 114

Note: Every effort was made to credit the photographs
used in this book. If there are any omissions, the
author here expresses his regrets and will supply miss-
ing credits, if brought to his attention, in future re-
printings.